THE DRUID ANIMAL ORACLE

WORKING WITH THE SACRED ANIMALS OF THE DRUID TRADITION

PHILIP and STEPHANIE CARR-GOMM

ILLUSTRATED BY BILL WORTHINGTON

Grange BOOKS

AUTHORS' ACKNOWLEDGMENTS

We would like to thank the following for their help, inspiration and guidance: Steve Blamaires of the Celtic Research Folklore Society and Anne MacDonald Coleman for their advice on the Gaelic names of the animals and their pronunciation; Elkheart for his many insights and suggestions on reading the draft manuscript; John and Caitlín Matthews for their fund of knowledge, so willingly shared; Chris Worthington and Daan Van Kampenhout for their ideas and enthusiasm; and Bill Worthington for his truly inspired and provocative artwork.

We are also grateful to Eligio Stephen Gallegos, whose work with animal imagery and symbolism has contributed so much to enriching psychotherapeutic practice; to the Folklore Society for their work in preserving so much of our native lore; to Woz and Chalkie for keeping us in touch with the animal world every day; and to Nuinn, as ever.

Published in 2001 by Grange Books
an imprint of Grange Books Plc
The Grange
Kingsnorth Industrial Estate
Hoo, nr Rochester
Kent ME3 9ND
www.grangebooks.co.uk

British Library Cataloguing-in-Publication date available on request

ISBN 1-84013-440-2

1 3 5 7 9 10 8 6 4 2

EDDISON • SADD EDITIONS
Editorial Director: Ian Jackson
Editor: Elisabeth Ingles
Creative Director: Nick Eddison
Designer: Pritty Ramjee
Line Drawing Artist: Anthony Duke
Production: Lindsey Scott, Charles James

The drawings on pages 12, 16 and 150 are copyright © Nicholas Mann and are reproduced by kind permission.

AN EDDISON • SADD EDITION
Edited, designed and produced by
Eddison Sadd Editions
St Chad's Court
148 King's Cross Road
London WC1X 9DH

Phototypeset in Adroit by
SX Composing Ltd, Rayleigh, England
Origination by Columbia Offset, Singapore
Printed and bound by L Rex Printing, China

CONTENTS

INTRODUCTION

Fruitful glen of fish-filled pools
Beautiful your rounded hills of wheat;
Remembering you causes me great distress,
Glen of bees and the horned wild ox
From "Deirdre Remembers a Glen," Irish fourteenth century

THE END OF LIVING AND THE BEGINNING OF SURVIVAL

In 1855 Chief Seattle warned the white settlers of America that "when the secret corners of the forest are heavy with the scent of many men" it would signal "the end of living and the beginning of survival." Those settlers came from a continent that had forgotten its native tradition in favor of a religion that taught man he must "be fruitful and multiply, and fill the earth and subdue it; and have dominion over the fish of the sea, and over the birds of the air, and over every living thing that moves upon the earth" (Gen.I.26).

Now, a century or so later, Chief Seattle's words call to us with an even greater urgency. We need to fight to preserve our forests and wildlife, and at the same time we need to connect to our spiritual roots so that we no longer feel alienated from the earth. To do this, we must turn to a study and practice of our native spirituality—which we are at last starting to remember. This book and card set represent one part of this remembering process, one way that we can connect again to a tradition that has never been lost—only forgotten. This tradition, that existed well before the advent of Christianity, is made up of many strands—Saxon, Norse, Greek and Roman amongst others—but prior even to these, the native Celtic and Druidic beliefs and practices lie at its foundations.

Looking, from the perspective of an earth religion such as Druidry, at the wasteland we have created in our search for profit and gain, we discover that there is no separation between our internal and external worlds. As the wilderness is eradicated, so some wilderness disappears in us too. As an animal becomes extinct, so something dies in us. As we abuse our external environment, we abuse our internal environment also. Nowhere is this more clearly demonstrated than in our destruction of the rainforest, extinguishing a thousand species each year, to produce more meat, whose over-consumption medical science has proved to be directly related to heart disease and certain cancers. With tragic symmetry we destroy the inner world of our bodies as we destroy the outer world that sustains and supports all life.

As you look through the animal cards, each of them calls to you. Some call only from the Otherworld. In Britain it is now the ghosts of bears and wolves, cranes and boar, that roam the hills longing to return. Their call, and the call of Druidry, is a call from the future, though, not the past. It is a call that urges us to unite again with all of creation, for there is still hope. It calls us to cease the madness of our alienation and destruction, and ally ourselves once more with all our relations—the stones and the trees, the birds and insects, the fish and the animals. Maybe then we can begin living again—not just surviving to suffer the consequences of our delusion that we are masters of all Nature.

THE DRUID CIRCLE

When we let go of believing we are superior, we open ourselves to the experience of living in the community of Nature—being a part of it, not separate from it. We are welcomed back into the circle we never really left, except in our delusion. The Round Table is made complete again. In Druidry, we come together in circles—seated in a circle around the fire, in a circle of stones or a grove of trees. And as we do this, we come to experience that we are in communion not just with our present-day physical companions, but with the spirits of the animals and trees, the stones and the stars, with our ancestors and our children and the children who will come when we have long passed into the Summerlands. Looking up into the night sky, we sense the animal spirits looking down on us—and we understand why the ancient Greeks named the circle of the con-stellations the zodiac—which means "the circle of living animals."

THE DRUID TRADITION—OUR FORGOTTEN HERITAGE

So much of our indigenous tradition seems lost that the work of compiling this book at first seemed daunting. But one of the exciting discoveries that we made as we created this book and oracle was that the knowledge of animal powers has by no means been lost—it has simply been neglected and forgotten. The material set down here does not represent **our** ideas about the animals or what they can bring us, instead it represents a part of that which the indigenous Celtic and Druidic tradition has gifted to us through more than 7,000 years of experience and learning.

With virtually every aspect of Druid teaching and practice we, as a culture, have been led to believe that hardly any vestige remains. And yet, simply put to one side rather than buried deep, there are the myths and stories, the folk customs and sayings, the stone circles and sacred sites, the Bardic remains and historical references that, pieced together and united with commonsense and intuition, reveal a practice and a teaching that can be and is being revived—all over the world.

OUR ANIMAL TEACHERS

Our ancestors revered every aspect of the natural world and considered each part of this world capable of being an ally, guide, and teacher. The Druid of today is able to draw inspiration, direction, and assistance from each realm of the natural world, but in the old days it was perhaps easier and less unusual—there were fewer "things" between us and the world of Nature, and the prevailing world-view saw every part of it infused with spiritual life and meaning. Animals in particular were revered for their qualities, and were seen as sacred to the Goddess or the gods.

A number of tribes or clans were reported to be descended from animals—such as the "cat-people" in Scotland and the "wolf-tribes" and "dog-heads" in Ireland. Some families were also said to have animal ancestry. The seal, for example, was the original ancestor of at least six families in Scotland and Ireland. Most tribes had their totem animals, clearly shown in their names, such as the Caerini and Lugi in Sutherland (People of the Sheep and People of the Raven), the Epidii of Kintyre (Horse People), the Tochrad (Boar People), Taurisci (Bull Folk), and Brannovices (Raven Folk).

Families too had totem animals, carried either in their name, their crest, or their family tradition. We are all familiar with English names which are clearly those of animals, such as Fox, and most of us know the animal that is related to those names of classical origin, such as Philip, from the Greek meaning "lover of horses." But many names in Gaelic come directly from the animal realm, and we have tried to mention as many as possible in Chapter Two. Learning that names such as Son of Fox or Little Wolf were common in our British native tradition makes us feel closer to our brothers and sisters of the native American tradition.

Our ancestors loved and respected animals so much they chose to be buried with them, to have them as guides and companions in the Otherworld. They wore their bones and teeth as charms. They used their skins for clothing and bedding, for their shields, drums, and bagpipes. They accepted their hide, horn, hoof, and meat as gifts, and made use of every part of the animal—even its excretions were sometimes used for healing. When they hunted, they asked the Goddess for permission first before they dared to take the life of any creature. The hunt itself was considered sacred, and a number of taboos surrounded it to protect both hunter and hunted.

The bond between our ancestors and animals was so extraordinarily rich that they found themselves in relationship not simply with lowly beasts, but with guardians, guides in this and the next world, healers, friends, and teachers. It is no wonder that they considered them sacred and the companions of the gods. It is only we, recent and two-dimensional humanity, that see in animals merely "lesser" creatures of inferior intelligence and little value, beyond that of a foodstuff.

ROOTED IN TIME

A reverence for animals and an awareness of them as teachers and guides is as old as humanity itself. The Drachenloch caves in Switzerland reveal altars dedicated to the Bear that are 70,000 years old. In the Lascaux caves in France, the extraordinary animal paintings and ceremonial bear's body statue are over 19,000 years old. Clearly animals were at the center of religious practice from the very earliest of times. In Britain, antlers nearly 10,000 years old, adapted for use as ritualistic headgear, have been found in a mesolithic settlement in Yorkshire.

Wearing animal skins, heads, and feathers was a way of identifying with them, of becoming them for a while, to partake of their powers and to receive divine inspiration. In Britain, the natives were still doing this in the seventh century AD—St. Augustine condemning "that most filthy habit of dressing up as a stag." In Ireland, the bard would wear a *tugen*—a feathered cloak made of "the skins of birds, white and many-colored . . . from the girdle downward, and of mallards' necks and crests from the girdle upward to the neck."

As well as dressing as animals, our ancestors sacrificed and buried them ritualistically. Any initial distaste at this behavior should be tempered with an awareness that millions of factory-farmed animals are now sacrificed daily, with no accompanying spiritual context—whereas the sacrifices and rituals of our ancestors involved small numbers of creatures and an intense awareness of the gift the animal was giving by being sacrificed. It seems that the animals were buried ceremonially as thanksgiving offerings in grain storage pits, when the pits were no longer required and were closed. Similar rituals must have occurred with the animals that accompanied the dead, or that were buried in shrines or sanctuaries.

The importance of animals in the religious life of our ancestors can also be seen in the fact that of the eight Druid festivals of the year, four of them, known as the Fire Festivals, are particularly related to the pastoral life of animal rearing and agriculture, and are known to have been observed for at least the last 7,000 years. Imbolc, on February 1st, is the time of lambing and calving and the first sowings. Beltane, on May 1st, signals the beginning of summer, when the herds are led up to the high pastures. Lughnasadh, on August 1st, marks the beginning of the harvest, and Samhuinn, on November 1st, signals the beginning of winter, when the animals are led down into the valleys, and any slaughter required to conserve stocks must be carried out.

SHAMANISM AND ANIMAL POWERS

Working with animal powers is a central feature of shamanism, and we can find many shamanic elements woven into the philosophy and practice of Druidry.

Michael Harner, a world authority on shamanism, speaks of the shamanic way as one which is best defined as a method to open a door and enter a different reality. Much Druid ceremony and meditation has as its goal journeying into other realities, and the word "Druid" is related to words meaning both "oak" and "door"—with the symbol of the door or gateway being central in Druidic teaching.

Joseph Campbell, the great mythographer, has shown that there are a number of key features which distinguish a shaman's art. These include: ritual dance, the possession of a wand or staff, ecstatic trance, the wearing of animal costume, identification with a bird, stag, or bull, becoming master of game animals and initiations, and the control of a magical animal or "familiar." Traces of possible ritual dances exist in the old folk dances, and there are numerous references to Druid wands and staffs and ecstatic or altered states in the literature of Druidry. The remaining features listed by Campbell all relate to animals, and are all known to exist within the Druid tradition. We have already discussed the wearing of animal costume, as stag or bird. Druids were often identified as animals: they were called adders or piglets, they were said to possess "crane, raven, or bird knowledge" or were given such names as Mathgen, meaning Bear-Born. Stags and bulls are particularly important in Druidry—the stag is a messenger from the Otherworld ridden by the sage Merlin, and the bull is sacred to the god Taranis, beneficent sky god of thunder and lightning and the oak tree. The bull figures prominently in the sacred music of Druidry—bronze rattles shaped like bull's testes were used ritualistically, as were the bronze horns that have been found throughout Britain and Ireland and which often look like bull's horns. When played with the circular breathing method used by didgeridoo players they sound like the roaring of bulls.

We find the image of the "master of game animals" in Celtic iconography and literature. Images of Cernunnos or of Lords of the Hunt can be seen in both Britain and France, and the striking image of the master of all animals appears in the Welsh *Mabinogion*. Finally, control of a magical animal or familiar is commonly related as an attribute of the witch in British folklore, with the hare, toad, and cat being cited as the most common familiars. There are many historical connections between Druidry and Witchcraft; more information on this can be found in *The Druid Way*.

THE CELTIC OTHERWORLD

Central to the world-view of the Druid is the belief that the material world we live in represents only one level or plane of existence. Behind or beyond this world lies the Otherworld, the world of powers and potencies, of spirits and forces which can guide and help us, if only we would recognize their existence and accept their reality.

Animals in particular are revered for their ability to bridge the gap between these two worlds. They can bring messages to us from the Otherworld, and they can act as our guides in that realm when we cast off our bodies in death. Because they have a spirit-form as well as a physical form, they can be our guardians and protectors even when they are not present physically. Although each animal has its own path into the Otherworld, a study of the animals described in this Oracle will show that they form certain groupings which are particularly suited to certain functions: some are most suitable as guardians and protectors, others as healers, guides, teachers, shape-shifters, or familiars. A guide to these different categories is given on page 163. It is interesting to note that the great majority of these animals are considered sacred to the Goddess.

INNER ANIMALS, POWER ANIMALS, TOTEM GUIDES

Working with the Animal Oracle can put us in touch with four different types of animal. First, it can open us to the beauty of the animal in the physical world, leading us to discover more about its life and ways. Secondly, it can put us in touch with our own "inner animals." Somehow animals act as ideal symbols or images of our deepest fears and urges, or of those parts of our psyche which have been denied or repressed or simply neglected. By welcoming and loving the animals which enter our awareness through the Oracle, in dreams and meditation and reverie, we enrich our inner world and discover a way of personal growth that is completely in tune with the natural world.

Thirdly, there are power animals. Druid tradition, in common with other indigenous ways, believes that animals also exist in spirit-form in the Otherworld, and sometimes these animals can visit us—to give us energy or healing, inspiration or advice. Because each of them carries a particular power, gift or "medicine," they are often called "power animals."

The fourth type of animal is known as a "totem." If we choose to work with power animals, we may find ourselves developing a special bond with one or more of them. We will sense their presence often in our consciousness—guiding, teaching, and helping us. We can then say that these power animals have become our "totems" or "familiars."

REDRESSING THE BALANCE—DANCING THE DREAM AWAKE

Our Judeo-Christian culture has taught us to be afraid of animals—our own animal nature and the animals of the wild. In teaching us to "subdue the earth" it also taught us to "subdue" our own instinctual selves. In this creation of a division between spirit and matter, mind and body, our inner animals were caged, frightened and forgotten. They appeared only in our dreams—they became the beasts that lurked at the fringes of our civilized world—werewolves and dangerous predators that symbolized the "bestial" urges of men too "civilized" to acknowledge the sacredness of the body and the animal.

But paradoxically, as long as we reject the animals within us, we can never be truly human. To regain our humanity we must embrace them—loving and coming to know each of them that exists in our hearts and souls. Working with the sacred animals can help us to do this—at the same time introducing us to a treasure-house of traditional wisdom which we can now reclaim and use for our own benefit, and for the benefit of all living beings.

CHAPTER ONE

ORACLES

Peer often deep within the pool of Fec
From the "Song of the Salmon-God" by W. P. Ryan

Goose and salmon on a Pictish stone from Morayshire, possibly sixth century

THE WATERS OF TIME

Life has often been compared to a river, whose flowing water represents the flowing of our lives toward an ocean of Oneness and Bliss. Using an oracle we attempt to look beneath the surface of the water, the surface of our lives, to observe its undercurrents, its depths, its hidden secrets. There we may be lucky enough to find the salmon of wisdom who can show us the truth that time is not linear.

It feels as if we are all walking a path that leads inexorably from the past to the future via the present, and yet mystical experience, the ancient wisdom traditions and now modern physics tell us that it only appears that way to our consciousness. The reality turns out to be far more extraordinary and wonderful—although impossible to grasp fully with our minds. Every so often, though, we will get glimpses of the truth that at some level linear time does not exist. This may happen in meditation, in sleep, or in a near-death experience, or time may play "tricks" on us—creating synchronistic experiences that amaze us with their impossibility or extreme unlikelihood in the normal course of events.

It seems that this time-free state holds the seed-bed, the impulses and dynamics which guide our passage through the world of linear time.

Oracles are devices which help us to gain access to this seed-bed deliberately and consciously. Through an oracle it is possible that we **may** get glimpses, insights, images, and ideas which will tell us about the dynamics, the "seeds," that lie behind events and experiences in our past, present, or future. BUT AN ORACLE CANNOT PREDICT A FUTURE EVENT. It can only point to possibilities and pitfalls, dynamics and options. It is all too easy to read an oracle and to take a word or idea given in its text as an omen or prediction. If you feel tempted to do this, please take some time to study this chapter before using the Animal Oracle. To use the Animal Cards effectively you need to know the difference between using an oracle and fortune-telling. Ralph Blum, discussing the oracular use of the runes, says that "they are not meant to be used for divination or fortune-telling. The disposition of the future is in God's hands, not ours. Rather, the Runes are a tool for assisting us to guide our lives in the present, for it is only in the present that our power can be exercised ... They are a system of guidance and self-counselling ... 'a compass for conduct.'"

Exactly the same can be said for the Animal Oracle. We should use it to discover not what will happen in the future, but what influences or tendencies **might** exist in our lives that need encouraging, understanding, or changing. The oracle then becomes a way of encouraging personal responsibility for our lives, rather than a resignation to our supposed fate. Just as in sailing a boat, the more we know about the tides and the weather, the better we are able to sail, so in life, the more information we have on its influences and dynamics, the more we are able to react to it in the most responsible and effective way.

THE BRIGHT KNOWLEDGE

Druidry recognizes that knowledge is neutral. It is how we use it that makes it good or bad, helpful or harmful. The Cauldron of Inspiration in Druidry provides both Bright Knowledge and Baleful Knowledge. It is our responsibility to use the knowledge we gain in creative, positive ways. This applies to all the knowledge we acquire—including that which comes from the use of an oracle.

Ovates, who are trainee Druids specializing in healing and working with the spirit of Time, in the past were also concerned with augury and divination. Augury is the making of predictions based on signs and omens, and many methods were used, including the interpretation of weather patterns, bird flight, and animal behavior, to predict the outcome of certain events. The Druid queen Boudicca (Boadicea), for example, let a hare run from her cloak just before her battle with the Romans. The direction in which it ran was interpreted as favorable to the British, who did indeed win the battle. *Neladoracht* was the Irish name for the Druid art of making predictions based on the observation of clouds, and similar techniques existed for observing signs and omens in fire or water.

Divination is a more sophisticated form of augury, and it is said that the Druids employed a form of divination based on a sacred woodland alphabet called Ogham, which used signs for each of the sacred trees and plants carved on sticks as symbols for a host of concepts. The sticks would then be cast on the ground and read. A modern adaptation of this system is given in Liz and Colin Murray's *Celtic Tree Oracle* and Nigel Pennick's *The Celtic Oracle*.

The Ovate used divination not only to plumb the subtle, intangible realms of time and the psyche, but also to discover tangible things, like water or metal, or objects lost or deliberately hidden. Dowsing to find a hidden water source, the Ovate would enact in the physical world the Druid search for hidden life and knowledge behind the veil of appearances.

THE DRUID ANIMAL ORACLE

The Animal Oracle, building on the accumulated wisdom of the past, is a new contribution to the ever-growing and changing tradition of Druidry. In particular we see it as a contribution to the Ovate stream of Druid teaching, in which the art of divination is informed and deepened by an understanding of psychology as well as traditional lore. The inspiration for it arose three years ago, when we were shown the Medicine Cards of Jamie Sams and David Carson during a workshop in America. Bringing a set back to England, we realized that Celtic and Druid animal lore could also be presented in the form of a card set. It seemed the perfect way to convey the richness of a tradition which is now being rediscovered. The Medicine Cards present primarily Native American animal teachings, but the first card spread suggested is a Druidic one, and its mention seemed a beautiful symbol of the rainbow bridge that connects our respective traditions. They have much in common: sacred circles, the honoring of the directions, a deep reverence for the natural world, a belief in animal guides, and an abiding sense that the land itself is sacred. There is even evidence that the Druids worked in sweat-lodges and we know that birds' feathers were used in ceremonial clothing and headdress. When we were in America some Native American teachers expressed the opinion that "white people" were taking their traditions from them, just as they had taken their land. "They should make connection with their own roots first," they told us. "Then they can come to us if they like, but first let them make peace with their own ancestors." While being wary of generalizing, because there are always exceptions, we believe they are probably right. Once we can feel fully at home in our own indigenous tradition, then somehow it is easier for us to relate to other traditions. Coming from a secure, rooted base we no longer have the feel of an outsider or a predator, and we can transcend the divisions of race and culture to feel truly at home in all traditions, with all of humanity.

In recognition of the deep bond that exists between the native traditions of all lands, we would like to offer this Animal Oracle as one means of helping people to connect to the richness of their spiritual heritage.

CHAPTER TWO

THE SACRED ANIMALS OF THE DRUID TRADITION

Horned figure, possibly Cernunnos, from the Gundestrup cauldron, Denmark, first century BC

The following pages present a summary of the Druid, Celtic and traditional teachings concerning twenty-nine animals and four dragons. Traditional lore can be found on more real and mythological animals than these, but we feel we have included the most important of them in our choice of thirty-three.

In addition to the thirty-three cards representing these animals, three blank cards are included for you to add your own favorite animals, should you find they are not among those in the deck. You might like to draw pictures of them on the blank cards, and the Further Reading list on page 176 may help you to locate traditional lore associated with them.

The cards have been drawn using the principles of sacred geometry, a science of great importance to the megalith-building pre-Celtic Druids, who employed it extensively in the building of stone circles. Each image incorporates the same use of a pentagram, circle, and square. The border of the animal cards conveys a message in Ogham—the tree-language of the Druids.

The names of the animals are given in English and Gaelic—mostly Scottish but with some Irish. Each animal has many different names in Gaelic, and we have tried to choose the most evocative. An approximate pronunciation guide is included in the quick-reference Index of Cards on pages 174–5.

The pages dealing with the tradition of each animal are designed to convey as faithfully as possible the traditional lore associated with that creature. The key-words and interpretations have been derived from a reading of that lore. Once you are familiar with the traditional lore and have a sense of being in touch with the animal in spirit, you may find yourself gradually developing your own interpretations.

The interpretations should not be read as predictions, but should be used to provide words of advice, and insights into the inner dynamics behind events.

Far from encouraging a fatalism, the interpretations should be used to empower you—to give insights that can help you correct imbalances and create more positive outcomes.

The animals are presented in a sequence starting with the Blackbird, who stands at the Gateway, the Place of Beginnings, calling us to adventure and change. Journeying to the four other Oldest Animals of Stag, Owl, Eagle and Salmon, we come to know animals that lead us deeper into the Otherworld, through a cycle of personal change that leads to turning to the outer world again, the empowerment of the four dragons and the concluding card of the Seal—the card of love and the necessity for choice in a world that is both joyous and challenging.

BLACKBIRD
Druid Dhubh

BLACKBIRD

Enchantment, The Gateway, The Inner Call

The card shows a blackbird sitting on a rowan tree. It is twilight and the first stars are just appearing in the sky. In the background we see the entrance to an enchanted cave. Druid Dhubh is the bird of both the gateway and the forge.

Druid Dhubh calls to us from the gateway between two worlds, urging us to follow a spiritual path or to become more self-aware. He calls to us in the twilight, showing us the path to Otherworldly secrets, pointing out the ways in which we can discover more about our hidden motivations and potential. There are times in life when it is important to concentrate on the outer world and your responsibilities in that world, but there are also times when you must attend to the haunting song of your soul which calls you to a study of spiritual truths, and to an exploration of the inner world through dreams and myths. In heeding Druid Dhubh's song, you will discover healing and new depths in your soul.

Drawn reversed, this card reminds you that the blackbird is the smith's bird, and his song may be calling you to work in the forge of your own heart—to create a life of passion and purpose. All four elements are used in metal-working, and to create a healthy and balanced life we must work with the power of the four elements, integrating and developing our minds and hearts, our instinct and our intuition. Just standing at the gateway between two worlds, without truly working in either, is a denial of our own power and responsibility.

The Tradition of the BLACKBIRD

May Day, season fair,
Perfect time of year,
The blackbird's song a poem
To the sun's first slender ray
Irish ninth century

One of the Gaelic names for the blackbird, Druid Dhubh, means the Black Druid. Druid Dhubh is a bird which sings beautifully and melodiously at twilight, and even later. Twilight is the shimmering time—a time of transition between one reality and the next. Such in-between times are considered especially significant in the Druid tradition. The blackbird sings to us as the world changes around us—as the time of daylight and consciousness and the concrete world gives way to the moon-time of the Unconscious, of the Otherworld. His song reminds us that these gateway-times are ones of great beauty and potential.

If we are able to follow Druid Dhubh's song we will be led to a place of depth and enchantment from which we may uncover secrets about ourselves and the world. There is an old tale in the French tradition which explains how the blackbird became black, and why it has a golden beak. Following a magpie's advice, a white bird entered an enchanted cavern to discover the priceless treasures of the Prince of Riches. Reaching a second, inner cavern the bird discovered a pile of gold dust. Plunging his beak into this dust, he was surprised by a demon guarding the treasure, who, belching fire and smoke, rushed headlong at him. As he flew out of the cavern, only just managing to escape the demon's clutches, he discovered that he was no longer white, but black, and that his beak was now a radiant golden color.

BIRDS OF THE DREAMTIME

The birds of Rhiannon are blackbirds, creatures partly of the Otherworld. In the old Welsh tale *Branwen Daughter of Llyr*, the hero Bran the Blessed and his seven followers are sung to by Rhiannon's birds as they live in a state of enchantment for seventy-two years—neither growing older nor being aware of time's passing. In another tale, *Culhwch and Olwen*, the giant Yspadadden Pencawr demands that the hero Culhwch capture Rhiannon's birds to entertain him, describing them as "they that wake the dead and lull the living to sleep." Here we see Druid Dhubh's function described: as a being who can send us into the dreamtime and who can speak with discarnate souls.

The counterparts in Irish tradition of the birds of Rhiannon are the birds of the goddess Cliodna who dwell on two Otherworld islands. They are depicted as being similar to blackbirds, but larger, with red plumage and green heads, laying crimson and blue eggs. A human who ate one of these eggs immediately grew feathers, which eventually washed away in water. These magical birds of the Otherworld would lull sick or wounded men to sleep, healing them with their sweet music.

Blackbirds are fond of rowan berries, one of the sacred trees in Druid tradition. Each berry carries a minute pentagram—a magical symbol of protection and power—that figures largely within Druid work, and that symbolizes good health, among many things. Eating these berries, the blackbird is able to connect us with his healing song to the balancing and regenerative powers of the Otherworld and the Unconscious.

THE OLDEST ANIMALS

The blackbird is one in a series of five totem animals central to the Druid tradition. In *Culhwch and Olwen*, the earliest tale to speak of King Arthur, the hero Culhwch is asked by the giant Yspadadden to find the Divine Youth Mabon. Together with some of Arthur's men, Culhwch goes on a journey to seek counsel of the Oldest Animals. They visit first the Blackbird of Cilgwri, since as far as they know he is the oldest animal in the world. "We are King Arthur's messengers," they say, "We have come to you since we know of no animal older than you. What can you tell us of Mabon?" He replies that when he first arrived at Cilgwri he found a smith's anvil, which he has worn entirely away, so long has he been there. He then admits that he knows nothing of Mabon, but that there is an animal older than he who may help them. They then visit in turn four other animals: the stag, the owl, the eagle and the salmon.

It is fitting that the blackbird should be the first in this totem cycle: for he stands at the gateway between two worlds, calling us with his song, lulling our waking minds to sleep and our psychic faculties into wakefulness. Then in turn we visit the still older animals until finally we reach the salmon of wisdom turning in the sacred pool.

Druid Dhubh is the blacksmith's bird—hinted at with the reference to the anvil in the story of Culhwch and Olwen. In Irish *ghoba-dhu* means both blacksmith and blackbird. Using rocks as anvils he cracks open snails' shells, and his plumage is as black as the smith's face and the iron that he forges. In Irish tradition the smith-god is Goibhniu, in Welsh tradition Gofannon. Brighid, too, is goddess of smiths—of fire and metal-working, poetry, inspiration and healing. The smith was an important figure in the old times—he forged the weapons and the wheels, the cauldrons and the plows. Harnessing the power of fire, and using it in combination with that of air and water and the ore extracted from the earth, he was seen to be working with all four elements to produce items vital to the well-being of the tribe. Druid Dhubh represents the Otherworldly smith—the master of fire who calls to us with his healing song—telling us that we can work with the air of our minds, the water of our hearts, the earth of our instincts and the fire of our spiritual passion to forge a new life for ourselves based on beauty, dignity and purpose.

HIND
Eilid

Subtlety, Gracefulness, Femininity

The card shows a white hind in the forest in late summer or early fall. Acorns hang heavy from the oaks. The hind calls us to follow her deeper into the forest. Standing in a shaft of sunlight, she appears so elusive we are not even sure if she is of this world.

Eilid brings us the gentleness and grace of the feminine principle. Whether you are male or female, opening to the qualities of the hind will enable you to achieve a greater degree of sophistication, subtlety and elegance—in the best possible senses of these terms.

Deer, and the white hind in particular, call to us from the Otherworld, from the realm of Faery, and invite us to look beyond the material, beyond the superficialities of life, toward the heart of things, toward the realm of causes rather than effects. Poised in moon- or sunlight, Eilid invites us to begin an exploration of the Otherworld, of the spiritual dimension of life.

Drawn reversed, this card may be warning you to be less self-effacing. Rather than adapting yourself, like a chameleon, to the perceived demands and expectations of those around you, you may need to become more assertive. You may also need to be wary of becoming preoccupied with the Otherworld. Our psychic life has its seasons, and at times it is good and balancing for us to explore the inner mysteries, but at other times it is important for us to focus our awareness on everyday life. You may have reached a time when an interest in the esoteric needs balancing with a period of outer activity. Do not worry that you will lose touch with the Otherworld, for the magical white hind will always be waiting for you at the edge of the woods, ready to guide you into the heart of the forest.

The Tradition of the HIND

The clear voice of the red-backed deer
Under the oak tree, high on the summit
Gentle hinds and they so timid
Lying hidden in your well-wooded glade
From "Deirdre Remembers a Glen," Irish fourteenth century

A female red deer is known as a hind, and this graceful animal was considered especially sacred by the Celts and Druids. In Scotland they are called "fairy cattle" and it is said that they are milked on the mountain tops by the fairies. Others believe that the hinds themselves are fairy women who have taken the form of deer.

There were at least three great hag-goddesses in Scotland who cared for these fairy cattle — one, called the *Cailleach-mor-nam-fiadh*, lived in the mountains on Jura, another, known as the *Cailleach mhor Chlibric* (The Great Hag of Clibric), protected the deer from hunters, and the third, the *Cailleach Beinn-a-bhric*, herded and milked them in the hills and forests. Verses of her milking song are still known to this day.

LUGAID AND THE HAG

The connection between hind and hag is also found in Ireland, in the story of how Lugaid became king. His father King Daire was told that whichever son of his was named Lugaid would inherit the throne. Because he could not bear to favor one of his five sons over the other four, he named each of them Lugaid. A Druid then told him that the son who caught a young hind would become the king. The five brothers set out hunting and eventually managed to hunt and eat a fawn. They then got lost in a snowstorm, and came upon an extraordinary house occupied by an ugly hag who asked each of the brothers to have intercourse with her. Four of them refused, but Lugaid Laigde, who had killed the fawn, agreed, and as he made love to her she turned into the most beautiful of women—symbolizing the goddess of the sovereignty of Ireland.

The Irish goddess of wild things was known as Flidhais—probably a divine huntress like Diana. Like the Great Hags of Scotland, she cared for deer cattle, and is known to some as the deer goddess.

Fairy women could be turned into deer by their rulers—a hundred *sidh* (fairy) girls met this fate when their queen had a fit of jealous rage. Mortals could become deer too: in the Fionn Cycle of tales from Ireland a Black Druid turns Fionn's future wife into a fawn. In the Welsh tale *Math*, from the *Mabinogion*, the brothers Gwydion and Gilfaethwy are turned into a stag and a hind for one year as a punishment. And in both the Scottish and Irish tradition, the mother of Ossian was turned into a hind through enchantment before she gave birth to the hero-poet.

"THREE AGES OF MAN, AGE OF DEER, THREE AGES OF DEER, AGE OF OAK TREE"

In the world of the Celts the deer was treasured for its hide: the skin of the hind was used to make women's clothes, and in the Irish *Cattle Raid of Cooley*, Cu-Chulainn's charioteer is described as wearing a "skin-soft tunic of stitched deer's leather, light as a breath." Archeologists conclude that the deer was probably the most common wild and hunted creature to be buried in the British ritual pits. At the major ritual site of Winklebury in Hampshire a pit containing a red deer surrounded by twelve foxes was unearthed, showing the importance the Celts attached to both these creatures.

The hind in particular was seen as a magical animal, capable of affecting men's lives and ways. The Scottish Lord of Kilmersdon's life was changed when he followed a magical white hind through the forest. After a mile or so it vanished, but such happiness came into his life from that moment that he built a Lady Chapel in the local church in gratitude. Another enchanted hind appeared before a hunter in the Highlands as a beautiful woman, holding the arrow he had just loosed. "I am the leader of my herd," she told the astonished hunter, "I am under *Fith Fath* (enchantment) and you must promise only to shoot at stags, not hinds." As he made his promise, the woman vanished, singing gently of her deer herd.

Further evidence of the way fairies protected their animals is shown in another Scottish tale of a hunter's dog who chased a white fairy hind grazing near Loch Ericht. The hind eventually led the dog into the waters of the loch, a gateway to the Underworld, and neither was ever seen again. In Ireland the story is told of Fionn mac Cumhaill who hunts a deer to the edge of a lake. Suddenly she turns into a beautiful girl who drops her ring in the water and asks Fionn to retrieve it. As he does so, he turns into a withered old man.

The Goddess, too, protects her deer. In another Irish tale, the Fianna were at one time hunting a fawn that led them to *Slieve-nam-Ban*, the Hill of the Woman. There she put down her head and vanished into the earth.

If our intention is to harm the animal realm, we should beware. But for those of us who hunt for knowledge, and not to kill, the shape-shifting hind will lead us ever deeper into the heart of the forest, ever deeper into encounters with the Otherworld, and with the realm of Faery.

STAG
Damh

STAG

Pride, Independence, Purification

The card shows a stag bellowing as it stands before a gateway of birch trees. According to Druid tradition, the birch is the tree of beginnings, and the stag is a creature from the beginning of Time. The gateway represents the place of transition from this world to the Otherworld, and the stag is often seen as an Otherworldly messenger. On the rock beside him is the carved figure of a man wearing antlers—he is the god Cernunnos, Herne the Hunter or Merlin. The plants in the foreground are all associated with the stag—pennycress (deer's pot-herb), mountain sorrel (deer's sorrel), common asparagus (deer's son's leek), and heathrush (deer's oats).

Damh brings us the qualities of grace, majesty, and integrity. Contemplating the stag can help you achieve a greater sense of poise and dignity. If you are ever confronted with a situation in which you feel vulnerable or under scrutiny, such as in a court of law or a public appearance, by attuning to the stag and asking for the protection of his spirit you will find yourself feeling calmer, stronger, and more dignified. The stag signifies independence too—both spiritual and physical. By drawing this card you will be able to find the strength to gain and maintain your independence. In Ogham, the Druid language of the sacred trees, the Stag is related to *Beith*, the birch tree and the number one. The birch is associated with the blessing of beginnings. It is auspicious to draw this card when contemplating new projects. The stag's connection with fertility and sexuality signifies that you will find a way to bring dignity, grace, power and integrity to your sexual life.

Drawn reversed, this card shows that you need to examine the degree to which your pride is helping or hindering you. Pride can be a valuable feeling when it helps you to give only of your best, but it can also block your development and enjoyment of life if it exists only to protect your feelings of vulnerability and inadequacy. Ask yourself whether your pride is serving you, and if not, see whether the qualities of the Stag can help you find integrity and dignity without the need for inappropriate pride. The stag-god, as Lord of the Hunt, is responsible for culling, which can be seen as a process of purification or sacrifice, maintaining a proper ecological balance. Drawing this card reversed may signify the need for sacrifice or purification in your life—perhaps through a letting-go of unnecessary possessions or emotional attachments, thereby helping you to gain independence and integrity.

The Tradition of the STAG

I am a stag of seven tines
The Song of Amergin

All deer are beautiful, graceful creatures, but stags are also majestic, by virtue of their magnificent antlers, made up of a number of spikes or tines. The antlers start to grow in the early summer and are fully developed by rutting time—the mating season in late autumn. Around the Druid festival time of Imbolc on February 1st they shed their antlers shortly before the birth of their young.

According to Welsh tradition, the stag is one of the five oldest animals in the world. We read of these animals in the story of *Culhwch and Olwen*, the earliest of tales to speak of King Arthur and his knights. In the story the young hero Culhwch falls in love with a giant's daughter, Olwen. The giant will give his daughter's hand in marriage only if Culhwch performs thirty-nine impossible tasks, such as to obtain the tusk of the chief boar and to capture the hounds of Rhymhi. But with the aid of Arthur and his men the tasks are accomplished—Culhwch is wedded to Olwen and the giant is beheaded.

One of the tasks set by the giant was to free Mabon, the Celtic Divine Youth or Son of Light, often equated with Apollo or Christ, from his Underworld imprisonment. Arthur chose four men to seek Mabon, including Gwrhyr Interpreter of Tongues, a man who could speak the languages of birds and beasts. To discover the whereabouts of Mabon they sought the oldest animal—the Blackbird of Cilgwri. But the blackbird directed them to a still older animal—the Stag of Rhedynfr on Fernbrake Hill. On reaching the hill, Gwrhyr said to the stag, "We are King Arthur's messengers. We have come to you since we know of no animal older than you. What can you tell us of Mabon?" The stag replied, "I know nothing of Mabon, but I will be your guide and will lead you to an animal that God made before me." He led the party to the Owl of Cawlwyd, who led them to the Eagle of Gwernaby who directed them finally to the oldest animal of all—the salmon, who took them to the castle where Mabon was imprisoned.

The stag is therefore one of five totem animals that are central to British tradition, the sequence of totem beasts from blackbird to salmon representing a journey that moves us ever deeper into the realm of the Otherworld.

DRESSING AS STAGS

For millennia humans have attempted to partake of the stag's power, dignity and connection with the Otherworld, by dressing as stags for ceremony and dance. In Britain this ritualistic activity is at least 9,500 years old. At Star Carr in Yorkshire a mesolithic settlement of this age has been excavated and a number of stag skulls complete with antlers have been found with hollowed-out insides and holes cut to make them easy to wear. The Celtic cauldron, found at Gundestrup in Denmark, shows Cernunnos or a Celtic shaman wearing such an antlered headdress, and human figures with antlered heads figure strongly in legend and folklore. Every year at rutting time in September, the Abbots Bromley Horn Dancers perform a dance with antlered headdresses. Such was the prevalence of similar activities throughout Britain that in the seventh century St. Augustine issued strict instructions that no one must indulge in "that most filthy habit of dressing up as a stag."

LORD OF THE ANIMALS

The Lord of the Animals was pictured as a man with antlers—the combination of human and animal characteristics signifying Otherworldly powers. Such a figure is seen in the legend of Herne the Hunter—an antlered man living in Windsor Forest, who is said to appear at times of national crisis—and in Cernunnos, the Celtic god of hunting. Traces of Cernunnos can be found in place-names such as Cerne Abbas in Dorset, site of a great ithyphallic giant carved in chalk on the hillside. Cernunnos is associated both with fertility (and hence sexuality), and with hunting and culling. He is seen as the Lord of the Wild Hunt, which carries the spirits of the dead to the Otherworld.

As well as traveling to the Otherworld with the Wild Hunt, the stag is also seen as a messenger from that realm, and for this reason he has often been associated with the festival of Samhuinn, October 31st to November 2nd, when the veil between this world and the next is drawn aside so that we can commune with the Ancestors. He brings with him power and knowledge of this other realm, and he carries on his back not only the King of Faery, but Merlin too.

BEAR
Art

Primal Power,
Sovereignty,
Intuition married with
Instinct

The card shows a bear standing by a cave entrance with a mace at its feet. Such a mace was found by archeologists near Stonehenge. It is midwinter—the time of *Alban Arthuan*, the "Light of Arthur," at the winter solstice. A crown lies in the foreground, and we see the Pole Star shining brightly above the constellation of the Plow, also known as the Great Bear or Arthur's Plow.

Art connects you with the very deepest of your ancestral roots. Here, at this level, you are in touch with the Primal Mother—the Bear goddess Artio who will defend you fiercely from all danger. You are connected also with the Bear god Artaois, the mighty warrior Arthur, the guiding Pole Star of the Great Bear. Your intuition will never fail you, if you will listen to it in the still darkness of the night. Working with the Bear gives you the opportunity to become a Spiritual Warrior—like Arthur. You can find the way to come into your power by marrying your strength with your intuition. Integrating your primal power with your intuition means uniting your star-power with your animal-power—and both are symbolized by Art, the Bear.

Chosen reversed, the bear card gives a clear warning that you must take care not to be overwhelmed by the ferocious mother, by the berserk warrior—by forces of anger and primal ferocity that, untempered with the human qualities of compassion and reason, can damage not only your own life, but those of others around you. Art brings a strong presence and great reserves of power, and with perseverance you will be able to integrate your spiritual, intuitive qualities with your primal, instinctual qualities.

The Tradition of the BEAR

With the blessings of the great bear of the starry heavens and the
deep and fruitful earth, we call upon the powers of the North
From Druid ceremony

The Arthurian legend, like a golden thread, connects the most sophisticated post-Christian forms of Druidic understanding with the very roots of Druidry in the Celtic and pre-Celtic past. Learning of the importance of the Bear in Druid tradition helps us to follow this golden thread back from Arthur to the very beginnings of humanity.

To understand the full significance of King Arthur in relation to the "Matter of Britain" and the Druid Mysteries, we need to understand the origin of his name. The name Arthur derives from the Celtic word Art, meaning bear, stone or God. Arthur is the "bearman"—as strong and powerful as a bear. The greatest compliment that could be paid to a hero in the Celtic tradition was to describe him as an *Art an neart*—a bear in vigor. But these attributions do not derive simply from the bear's legendary strength and ferocity. Of all the animals sacred to the Druids and Celts, and indeed many other European and North American races, the bear seems to have been among the very first of animals to be honored and revered.

THE BEAR CULT

The finding of stone altars and significant caches of bear bones at Drachenloch in Switzerland shows us that Neanderthal man revered the cave bear as Master of all Animals as far back as 70,000 years ago. In the Lascaux caves in France we find, dating from 17,000 BC, the headless model of a bear which for ceremonies was almost certainly draped in fur with a bear's head attached. The bear is therefore truly one of the primal totems, if not **the** primal one. Joseph Campbell goes so far as to suggest that the Bear Cult was older than shamanism by many centuries.

Bear-cult sites, votive statues and ritual jewelry have been found widely distributed over Celtic territory, and we find the Celts, and hence the Druids, honoring the bear goddess Artio or Andarta ("powerful bear") and the bear god Artaois, Ardehe or Arthe. An image of Artio has been found in Berne (Bear City) as has a "den of bears"—used for cult practices. A sixth-century BC altar dedicated to the bear god Ardehe has been found in the French town of St. Pé-d'Ardet (from St. Père *Ardehe*) which lies in the "Valley of the Bear"—the Vallée de *l'Our*se—not far from *Lour*des. Bear pelts were favored for clothing, and the late Iron Age chieftain whose burial was uncovered at Welwyn in Hertfordshire was found lying on bearskin.

THE PRIMAL POWER OF THE BEAR

Neolithic man hunted the brown bear, and it was found in Scotland until about the end of the eleventh century. Bears' teeth were considered potent charms and several jet bear amulets have been found in North Britain. Due to its extraordinary ferocity, the Caledonian bear, as it was called, was a valuable export to Rome. Certainly, the ferocious bear was invoked before going into battle—with bearskins often being worn. Identifying with bear-power, the warriors went "ber-serk."

The place of honor given to the bear in the Druid tradition degenerated with the coming of Christianity, and was perverted into the pastime of bear-baiting. In Tudor times, every important town had its own bear, bear-baiting arenas were commonplace, and there was even the official post of "Master of the Queen's/King's bears."

Bears toured the country decorated with ribbons or flowers, often blinded to maintain obedience, and this tradition is continued to this day by gipsies in the Balkans.

The need, rooted in its pagan past, for each community to have its own bear can be seen as late as the seventeenth century, when we learn that at Congleton in Cheshire the citizens decided to use the money set aside for a new bible to purchase a replacement for the town bear which had just died. Hence the rhyme:

Congleton rare, Congleton rare,
Sold the Bible to pay for a bear.

We still talk about a child needing to be "licked into shape." This curious phrase derives from a belief that a bear cub was born a formless mass of flesh which the mother then licked into shape. An equally fantastic notion was held with regard to a bear's paws. It was believed that they secreted a substance which, when licked, could nourish the bear through the long winter months. Even today in China, live bears have their paws severed for their supposed medicinal value.

The importance of the Bear in Druid tradition is shown by the fact that Arthur is symbolically attributed in Druid ceremony and teaching to the Pole Star, above the constellation of the Great Bear, sometimes known in Celtic stories as Arthur's Plow. When all is dark to us, when the time of the longest night is upon us at the Winter Solstice, we turn to Arthur, the Pole Star, as our only guide. Arthur then becomes our intuition—our only guide when our reason and senses cannot help us. For this reason the Winter Solstice is known as *Alban Arthuan*—the Light of Arthur.

In this way, primal shamanism from the time of earliest man connects with the later Christian-influenced Druidry of the Arthurian Mysteries through the image of the Bear—who has become both star and animal.

FOX
Sionnach

Fox

Diplomacy, Cunning, Wildness

The card shows a fox starting to walk across a frozen lake. In Scotland there is a folk saying: "When the Feast of Brighid (Imbolc) is past, the fox won't trust his tail to the ice." As far away as Thrace, country folk would only cross ice if a fox had done so first. In the foreground we see *Ngetal*, the reed, and *Tinne*, holly, two of the sacred plants of the Ogham alphabet. Under the snow lie foxglove and fox-weed.

Sionnach is a fine, graceful creature who typifies the beauty and harmony of the natural world. Working with the power of the fox, you will know when it is time to come out into the open and be counted, but you will also know when it is time to remain silent, to keep your own counsel. With others you will be able to be diplomatic, and one of the attributes of the fox is being "strong in council." One of the hardest things, if you are a person working with "fox-power," is to ensure that your skill and diplomacy do not become dishonesty or slyness. Remaining silent, or becoming invisible so as to watch the unfolding drama, is an asset that can bring with it its own special culpability, if it is not tempered with wisdom.

Drawn reversed, this card may be warning you to be careful not to use your cleverness dishonestly. The knowing or kenning of the fox can easily become cunning which turns into conning. The reversed card may also mean that you are coming into contact with that part of you which feels a victim. In the past, the fox was hunted for its beautiful fur, but the hunt was considered sacred. From the moment weapons were forged, the hunt was dedicated to the Goddess, and her permission was sought before the hunter would dare take the life of any animal. More recently, the fox has become a symbol of the innocence and beauty of the natural world being destroyed by man's cruelty. If you feel you are at the mercy of circumstances, or are being unfairly or cruelly treated, take a lesson from the fox and "lie low" for a while. Concern yourself with family and home, and develop your skills of mediation and diplomacy.

Most of the animal names used contemptuously come from a patriarchal culture and hence are applied to women (bitch, cat, cow, and shrew for example) but the insult of "vixen" includes an erotic connotation—accusing a woman of being a vixen suggests she is cunning and ill-tempered, but also sexy. The term "foxy lady" conveys this idea, but in a more positive light. Having chosen this card reversed, it may be that you need to discover how you can show the wild and erotic side of your character—the Wildman or Wildwoman in you—in the most creative way.

The Tradition of the FOX

My blessings on the cunning ones
For hunting down the sheep
Duncan ban MacIntyre

The Scottish bard MacIntyre blesses the foxes for their work in keeping the sheep from destroying the landscape that he loves.

Although the ancient Celts kept sheep in large quantities, primarily for their wool rather than their meat, it was much later that sheep farming took on industrial proportions with vast areas of land being cleared to make way for massive flocks.

Whereas the sheep is a symbol of domestication and civilization, the fox represents wildness and wilderness. Sheep graze openly on the downland, whilst foxes are adept at concealing themselves, although they can live in all sorts of terrain—both cultivated and uncultivated, including sea-cliffs and sand-dunes, and even on derelict sites in large cities. Their ability to hide and move swiftly and invisibly through the forest, together with their reputation for stealing domestic animals such as chickens, has associated them with ideas of cunning and trickery. But cunning and kenning come from the same Old English root. To ken means to know or to see and recognize at a distance—as in "It's beyond my ken," which means "It's beyond my knowledge." The fox is seen as crafty and cunning, but behind this we sense that he is actually kenning— knowing and in possession of clear vision.

SON OF FOX—STRONG IN COUNCIL

The Celts and Druids clearly admired the skill of the fox. A Celtic chieftain of Gaul was called Son of Fox, *Louernius*, and this name has also been found on some third-century AD pewter tableware from Berkshire and in a fourth-century AD shrine in the Cotswolds. Due to his skills in diplomacy, Ua Leochann, a king of Gaileng in Scotland, who died in 989, was known as *An Sionnach*, the Fox.

In 1984 the two-thousand-year-old body of a man who had been garrotted was found in the Lindow Moss peat bog near Manchester. The evidence of his fox-fur armlet, the traces of mistletoe pollen in his gut, and his death by three causes, led the Celtic scholar Dr. Anne Ross to suggest that he too was called Louernius, and that he was a Druid prince ritually slaughtered to protect Ireland from the Romans.

Another association of royalty or chieftainship with the fox comes from Westmeath in Ireland where the family of O'Caharney or O'Kearney, who were once chiefs of Taffia, were called Sinnachs or Foxes.

But the name *sinnach* or *sionnach* is only one of many names for the fox. Another name, *reynard* (from the Norman-French), means "strong in council"—a term which points to our ancestors' recognition of the positive rather than negative qualities of the fox. *Sionnach* is the word for the reed of the bagpipe—perhaps because a vixen's wail could sound like a bagpipe playing.

THE FOX'S PELT

The reddy-brown coat of the fox, with its dash of white on the tail, was highly prized by the Celts for clothing and perhaps for bedding too. The classical writer Diodorus Siculus mentions that "their custom is to sleep on the ground upon the skins of wild animals." Bearskin would have probably been the favored pelt due to its thickness, and we know that the pelts of dogs and wolves were used, particularly in Gaul.

Although foxes were hunted for their pelts, there is good evidence to suggest that such hunting was a ritualized activity and that the fox itself was considered sacred. Fox-hunting is depicted on the rock art of the Camonica Valley in Italy. This valley is rich in carvings dating from the Neolithic to the Iron Age, and together with the rock art found in Scotland, provides valuable insights into our ancestors' way of life. Ritual burials excavated in France and England have shown the fox to be prominent. The great ritual enclosure at Aulnay-aux-Planches in Marne yielded the remains of a sacrificed dog, fox and young bear. At an Iron Age ritual pit at Winklebury in Hampshire a red deer and twelve foxes were buried. Deer and fox were found together again in the shrine at Digeon (Somme) and remains of foxes have also been found in the Gaulish sanctuaries of Mirebeau and Ribemont.

In common with the otter, the fox is said to carry a magical pearl, which brings good fortune to whoever finds it.

BOAR
Torc

BOAR

The Warrior Spirit, Leadership, Direction

The card shows a boar in the forest. In the foreground lies a bronze carnyx, with its mouth in the form of a boar's head. Such a battle-trumpet has been found in Grampian, Scotland. By the path, and also from Scotland, is the Boar Stone, beside which all Pictish kings took their oaths. To one side we also see the discarded bronze helmet of a warrior, complete with boar crest—as found in Powys, Wales. In the foreground grow mugwort, dandelion, and wild asparagus.

Torc can open you to the warrior spirit, helping you to find your direction in life. A wild and powerful animal, he calls you into the forest to discover a secret about yourself and about the world. The ritual boar-paths that exist in Wales, Cornwall, Ireland and Scotland exist in the Inner World too, and if you follow them you will come face to face with an animal embodying the wild and untamed power that lives within each one of us. Stare closely at him and you

will discover he is a representative of the Goddess—his skin can
heal you, he can inspire you to write music and poetry, his primal
power can make you leader or chief. See if you can use your wildness and your energy for genuine acts of heroism in a world that
longs for insight and healing.

Drawn reversed, this card may mean that you have lost your sense
of direction. There is a close connection in tradition between madness and pigs and boars. At a playful level this "folly" is expressed
by the morris dancer who beats the audience with a pig's bladder—
also used as a football. But at a more serious level, those who were
mad were often made to act as swineherds. Merlin, in his period of
madness, talks to pigs, and within this image is conveyed the concept that madness and insight are closely allied. Sometimes we
have to go through a period of "breakdown" so that something
wider and deeper can enter into our lives. The Boar is the emissary
of the Terrible Mother—who is also the Initiator. Sometimes a
period of destruction must precede a period of creation, of rebirth.

The Tradition of the BOAR

The tusk of Ysgithyrwyn Chief Boar I must have, wherewith to
shave myself
From the "Tale of Culhwch and Olwen"

In the Celtic tradition, the boar symbolizes raw power, which is
often destructive but which can be used and channeled by the
hero—the warrior. Many terrifying and magical boars are depicted
in the old tales. In the Irish Book of Invasions there is the Orc
Triath, a huge and destructive boar. In the Fionn Cycle of stories
there is Formael—massive and vicious, he kills fifty soldiers and
fifty hounds in a single day. In the Welsh tale of *Culhwch and
Olwen*, two boars play a central role. Ysgithyrwyn, Chief Boar, and
Twrch Trwyth must both be defeated by the hero Culhwch ("pig-
run"). From the Chief Boar the tusk will be used as a razor to shave
a giant, and from Twrch Trwyth the comb and scissors between its
ears will be used to cut the giant's hair.

The comb is a symbol that has been associated with the boar for thousands of years. The ancient rock-carvings in Scotland depict both combs and mirrors beside boars, and these symbols provide the clue that the boar is in fact sacred to the Goddess—despite the fact that it can also symbolize aspects of male aggression and sexuality. The Jungian Erich Neumann suggests that "The Great Mother is the sow that farrows and the boar that kills." The terrifying and destructive Irish boar Formael confirms this association with the feminine when we read that he has neither ears nor testicles. And in Scotland women would traditionally give birth at the Boar Stone, placing their bare feet on the stone to absorb its power. The theme of the boar as secretly or inwardly feminine is further confirmed when we learn that the White Boar of Marvan, in Irish tradition, acted as muse to his master—inspiring him to write music and poetry.

The boar's wildness and destructiveness were used by the Celts to arouse their fierceness and to terrify their enemies. The boar was used as an emblem on helmets, and as a mouthpiece on battle-horns. The snarling open mouth of the boar's-head trumpet found in Grampian held an articulated wooden tongue which would vibrate when blown—undoubtedly making a horrendous and frightening noise. The boar was also depicted on swords and bronze shields, and here these images are used to invoke the power of the boar to protect the warrior and to instill in him its supernatural vigor and fierceness.

At great feasts, the best joints of meat were given to the champion of the day—and these servings were known as "The Hero's Portion." Boars, however, were not generally eaten.

THE DIVINE HUNT

The classical writer Arrian mentions the fact that the Celts always invoked the blessing of the gods before they went hunting, and that they made offerings in exchange and thanksgiving for the creatures they hunted. At the time of the hunter-goddess's birthday a domestic animal was sacrificed in exchange for the wild one killed in the hunt, and this, together with the first fruits of the hunt, was offered to the goddess.

The hunt was seen as more than just an opportunity for sport; from the moment the weapons were forged, it was considered a sacred act, in which the hunter and the hunted entered into a special relationship. The Hunt became the symbol or metaphor for the journey of the Spirit—in which both life and death play their part, and in which healing is found through the process of hunting. Hunting and healing seem unrelated activities, but the archeological finds at the healing sanctuaries at Lydney in Gloucestershire and Nettleton Shrub in Wiltshire show that the Celts linked the two concepts. The perception that the death of one animal gave life to another led the Celts to connect the shedding of blood with ideas of rebirth, healing, and renewal.

Embarking on the boar hunt we are called to renew ourselves. In the forest is the ritual boar-path. First we must ask for the blessing of the gods or the Goddess. And then, if we dare to follow the path into the darkness, we will come face to face with the terrifying figure of the Wild Boar. In reality the boar has two tusks, but in our hunt which has taken us into the Otherworld he may have just one shining white tusk, like Chief Boar, or he may have three tusks— just as Otherworldly bulls can have three horns. If we face him with courage he will allow us to absorb some of his power. As we open to this primal life-force, we may see first the mouth of the Underworld, the Cave of Cruachan. From the mouth of the cave numberless pigs of death emerge, which we can neither count nor destroy. But if we stand our ground, the image will fade and we will see the single boar before us no longer as a snarling animal, but as Taliesin saying "I have been a wild boar," as Amergin saying "I am a courageous wild boar," and then as the Druid of the goddess Ceridwen—*Gwydd Hwch*—Boar of the Trees.

HAWK
Seabhac

HAWK

Nobility, Recollection, Cleansing

The card shows a merlin, the smallest of the hawks, perched on a cliff above a beach, on which burn two Beltane fires. It is dawn, and in the foreground to the left hawksbeard is growing, with common hawkbit to the right. The hawk's mate, a female merlin, flies high above the beach.

Seabhac brings the ability to see your life in perspective, to free you of unnecessary "baggage" and to connect you to your ancestral roots. See if you can take some time out of your daily routine to survey your life calmly and to see events in context. The Hawk can help you to recollect the missing pieces of the jigsaw you will be trying to assemble and he will help, too, to spot the details which are significant. When you have a sense of your roots and of the breadth of your life, you will start to feel pride and a growing sense of nobility and stature. Once you know where you have come from and where you are going, your life will be filled with inspiration and enthusiasm, you will sense a new day dawning, and you will be able to make decisions with confidence.

Drawn reversed, this card suggests that you could be paying too much attention to detail. Being precise and "hawk-eyed" can be valuable, but taken to its extreme and without a wider overview, it can lead to cruelty. High ideals if not balanced with a sense of humility lead to arrogance and ultimately a denial of the heart. Be careful not to get carried away by the justness of your cause, while forgetting to take into consideration the feelings of others.

The Tradition of the HAWK

I am a hawk on the cliff
The Song of Amergin

In the Druid tradition an inspired bard was said to possess "bird's knowledge." Druid shamans would dress in cloaks of bird feathers to perform certain ceremonies, and divination would be practiced by observing the flight of birds. In trance, the Druid would enlist the aid of his bird spirit-ally to fly to other realms, or would transform himself into a bird on the inner planes to accomplish a certain task. Each type of bird represents different qualities, evokes different experiences, and has different gifts for the Druid: the eagle brings renewal, the wren humility, the swan grace, the raven initiation. The hawk, whether kite, harrier, merlin, goshawk, or sparrowhawk, can give nobility and stature, dignity and pride.

The hawk has long been associated with chivalry and nobility. Hawks were used for sport by the privileged from the earliest days, and by medieval times a hierarchy of birds had been established. Kings, princes, dukes and earls could use falcons for hunting, yeomen used goshawks. The merlin, the smallest hawk, was used by ladies, while the sparrowhawk was used by the priest.

THE SEARCH FOR THE GRAIL
We see evidence of the connection between chivalry and the hawk in Welsh tradition. In the old tale *Pwyll Prince of Dyfed*, from the

THE DRUID ANIMAL ORACLE

Mabinogion, Pwyll exchanges gifts of horses, grayhounds and hawks with the King of Annwn, the Otherworld. King Arthur's nephew, Gawain, who challenged the Green Knight, is called in Welsh Gwalchmai—the Hawk of May. And Galahad, the son of Lancelot, was called Gwalch-y-Had—the Hawk of Summer. Because of its ability to soar high in the air, the hawk is considered a solar bird and therefore provides a fitting name for these knights who typify the best qualities of courtliness and nobility—they are male solar heroes in quest of the feminine grail.

The quest for the grail—for healing, completion and illumination—leads back to the source of all things. Traveling into our past, exploring our myths and traditions, leads us to discover that we are far richer than we ever supposed. We discover our heritage, our roots in the ancestral wisdom that still lives within our psyches and our culture. The hawk is a symbol both of the dawn and the freshness that a new day brings, and of the power of recollection—which enables the seeker to travel back through the pathways of time to discover their heritage, their birthright.

THE GREAT ANCESTOR

The hawk is a powerful ally in this quest. According to Irish tradition the hawk is one of the oldest animals in the world. In a riddling dialogue with Fintan, it shows a depth of knowledge stretching back almost to the beginning of time. In the folk-tale *The Hawk of Achill*, we learn that the coldest night ever known was one Beltane eve. Ages later the world was struck by another night of severe cold. Killing the fledgling he found there, the Hawk of Achill took shelter in an eagle's nest. When the mother returned, she began to feed the hawk, mistaking it for her fledgling. Almost freezing in her nest, she complained that the world could never have been so cold, but the hawk said that he could remember a much colder night. "But how could you remember such a time, when you were only hatched a month ago?" the incredulous eagle asked. "If you don't believe me," replied the hawk, "ask the blackbird at the forge if I speak the truth." The blackbird had worn an iron bar almost in two with his beak, but he could not remember a colder night. The eagle then flew to an ancient stag who had lived for over four thousand years and whose antlers had furnished sufficient material to fence a one-acre field. He told her to ask the Blind Salmon of Assaroe. On reaching the salmon and asking him if he could remember a colder night than this, the old fish replied that he could indeed. "It was so cold," he said, "I was frozen into the ice of this pool. The Hawk of Achill swooped down at me and pecked out my eyes, and that is why I am blind to this day. I'll bet you that fledgling of yours is none other than the Hawk of Achill himself." Flying back in fury, the eagle returned to an empty nest.

In the Irish *Book of Invasions*, Fintan, the great ancestor, becomes at one stage a hawk, as well as a salmon and an eagle. In these transformations, he reveals himelf as the prototypical Druid shaman who preserves the memory of the tribe and the ancestral spiritual knowledge by being able to travel back in time to learn the wisdom that is held by the very oldest animals.

The story of the Hawk of Achill reminds us that hawks are powerful and potentially dangerous birds—even the smallest of them, a merlin, can kill a partridge with one pounce. They will commonly feed on rats, hares, rabbits and mice. And one type of hawk, the magnificent kite, often mentioned in Celtic poetry and proverbs, could frequently be seen in the old days helping to clear the towns and villages of garbage as it scavenged amongst the offal and carrion.

Their ability to hunt vermin rendered them allies to the courtly sportsman; as the far-seeing hunters of the air they were the allies also of the Druid who wished to explore the spirit-world and who wished to heal by ridding the soul of impurities which the spirit-hawk could seek out for him. It is no wonder that in popular mythology it was considered lucky to see a hawk first thing in the morning.

DOG
Cù

Guidance, Protection, Loyalty

T he card shows a deer-hound similar to the hound portrayed in the bronze figure found at the third-century
shrine of the healer-god Nodens at Lydney, Gloucestershire.
Another healing sanctuary at Nettleton Shrub in Wiltshire
was dedicated to Apollo Cunomaglus—the Celtic "Hound-
lord"—showing that the dog was strongly associated with
healing. It is a bright summer's day, with the dog-rose, dog-
daisy, dog-violet and dog-periwinkle all in flower. These hot
days of July and August are called the dog-days because at
this period the Dogstar Sirius rises and sets with the sun. We
see a pool beside the dog, for there is a deep symbolic connection between the dog and water.

Cù brings guidance and protection, acting as a loyal companion
and friend on your journey in both this life and the next. In the
Druid tradition the dog is seen as the Guardian of the Mysteries. As

such, he can be fierce, but if our intentions are good, then Cù will lead us over the threshold through the darkness and the waters of the Unconscious toward the shimmering realm of the Goddess.

The time may come when you need to act with the spirit of Cù—to defend your values or protect that which you hold sacred. Faithfulness, trust, and loyalty are vital ingredients of close relationships, and the time may have come for you to focus on these qualities—to develop them gradually in yourself and to appreciate them in others.

Drawn reversed, this card urges you to examine the degree to which you or those around you may be lacking in faithfulness or loyalty. Ask yourself to what extent you value these qualities in your friends and lovers, and to what extent you and they express these values. If you find it difficult to keep friendships, Cù as your ally will help you to develop the qualities of selflessness and trust that will nurture close relationships. But remember that sometimes loyalty and faithfulness can be inappropriate—a dog is often submissive and anxious to please even a cruel owner.

The Tradition of the DOG

Fierce, with their bristles up, my gallant dogs!
That in their speed outstripped the howling storm
From the Ossianic poem "Manos"

The dog is a powerful guardian: Celtic ambassadors were accompanied by dogs which acted as bodyguards, and in recognition of their role as protectors, the term "dog" became a title of honor given to chiefs and warriors, heroes and champions, whose names were often prefixed by "dog"—such as Cu-Uladh and Cu-Chulainn. Even certain kings were honored in this way, such as the British kings Cunoglasus (Tawny Dog) and Cunobelinn (Dog of the god Beli).

In Ireland there are tales of the dog-tribes—"men with the heads of hounds"—and the inhabitants of Connaught are said to be descended from them. The *Concheannaich* (Dog-heads) were a similar tribe who lived at Moygonihy in Kerry.

GUARDIAN OF THE MYSTERIES

The dog as champion guards more than human lives and livestock. He is the guardian animal of roads and trackways, of crossroads and gateways. Here we begin to glimpse the role of the dog as guardian of the Mysteries, of the Underworld. English folklore is replete with tales of the Black Dog—a phantom dog that presages death or patrols the networks of ancient trackways and roads, and other places of transit. Death represents a moment of transit from one place to another, and the dog stands at these threshold places as guardian and protector. Just as the dog would guard its master from harm in the physical world, so in the Otherworld would the dog protect and guide the soul of the dead. For this reason, figurines of dogs often accompanied Celts in their graves, and favorite dogs were buried with their keepers. Later, dogs came to be depicted on gravestones for the same reason. Just as a faithful and loyal dog can guide a blind man through the obstacles and dangers of the physical world, so can the dog as a spirit-ally guide us safely through the Otherworld.

The loyalty and faithfulness of the dog provide us with a model of devotion and service which is free of the complexity and ambivalence that characterize human relationships. The contrast between the innocence and selflessness of a dog's loyalty and the burden of guilt we carry as a result of our human intelligence and feelings is powerfully conveyed in the Welsh story of Prince Llywelyn and his dog Gelert. One day, when the prince had to lead a raiding party, he left Gelert to guard his baby son who lay asleep in his tent. When he returned, he found the tent collapsed, with Gelert seated beside it, covered in blood. In despair and fury he ran his sword through the dog, only to hear a cry, and to find his son alive and well, with the carcase of a huge wolf slain by the faithful Gelert lying nearby.

DOGS AND HEROES

Many heroes were accompanied by a dog—King Arthur's dog was known as Caball, and the Irish god-hero Lugh had a magic hound that was unconquerable in combat, and which could turn spring water into wine. During a forest exile and separation from his beloved Isolt, Tristan's faithful dog Houdain kept him alive by catching game.

The life of the great Ulster hero Cu-Chulainn is intimately bound up with the dog as totem animal. As a boy, arriving late at a celebration held by Chulainn the Smith, he found the gates of the enclosure guarded by the smith's savage hound. The dog sprang at him, but he grabbed it by the throat and smashed it against a pillar. Chulainn was deeply upset by the loss of his dog, but the boy promised to rear a puppy for him, and to act himself as guardian-hound of the household until the dog was full-grown. During his life he became a mighty warrior, and was named Hound of Chulainn by Cathbad the Druid. He was also known as the "Hound of the Bright Deeds," the "Hound of the Sweet Discipline," and the "Hound of Ulster." His downfall occurred when three old hags persuaded him to eat some of the dog-meat they were roasting on spits of rowan. Once he had broken his obligation never to eat the meat of his totem animal, his power rapidly declined and he was soon overcome by Lugaid, the son of Cu Roi macDaire.

Another great hero, Fionn mac Cumhaill, was surrounded by dogs who had been humans—his aunt Turen was turned into a dog by a fairy and his own two dogs, Bran and Sceolang, were once his nephews. Bran's legendary exploits, recounted in the Irish Fionn cycle and the Scottish tales of Fingal, have made him a dog-hero.

The connection between dogs and water is ancient. Many goddesses of the Celts and Druids were depicted with dogs as companions. Lakes, pools and the sea were all seen as gateways to the Otherworld, and as guardians and guides of this realm dogs were often depicted as going into the sea. By entering the sea or a lake in legend, the dog is seen as entering the magical Otherworld of the Unconscious, of dreams, of life-after-death in which all things are renewed and healed and in which we find immortality.

OWL
Cailleach-oidhche

Detachment, Wisdom, Change

The card shows a tawny owl in an oak tree covered in ivy. A full moon shines between the winter-bare branches of the trees. Hung on the tree are votive offerings to the Cailleach (crone or hag-goddess) of a Celtic head and the spiral of death and rebirth.

Cailleach-oidhche teaches us the wisdom of turning a disadvantage into an advantage. For most birds, the coming of darkness renders it impossible for them to feed, but the owl's exceptional hearing enables it to pick out and swoop on unsuspecting prey during the night. Twilight has been described as owl-light, and going for a quiet walk in the woods at this shimmering time of twilight is an excellent way to develop a sensibility to the Otherworld and the inner soul of Nature. You may feel drawn to a study of esoteric lore or clairvoyancy. Working with the owl as your ally will help you to do this.

Drawn reversed, this card may indicate that you need to be wary of withdrawing too much from the world. An ability to be detached and discerning is an asset, unless it becomes a defence against being fully alive with all the vulnerability this entails. Perhaps there is not such a need for secrecy or holding back. The owl can signal a time of change, of initiation, of new beginnings. It can portend the death of one thing, but also the birth of another. An old Sussex saying is "When owls whoop at night, expect a fair morrow." Expect a bright dawn and it will surely come.

The Tradition of the OWL

I am coeval with the ancient oak
Whose roots spread wide in yonder moss,
Many a race has passed before me,
And still I am the lonely owl of Srona
Domhnull Mac Fhionnlaidh

The Bardic colleges survived in Scotland until the beginning of the eighteenth century. A collection by Maclean Sinclair entitled *Gaelic Bards from 1411 to 1715* includes the poem "The Hunter and the Owl," one of whose verses is quoted above.

The idea that the owl is ancient—that "many a race has passed before me"—is also found in Welsh tradition. In the story of *Culhwch and Olwen*, the earliest of tales to speak of King Arthur and his knights, Gwrhyr Interpreter of Tongues—a man who could speak the languages of birds and beasts—together with three others, goes on a journey to seek the Oldest Animals, in the hope that they will know where the Divine Youth Mabon can be found. They come first to a blackbird, who directs them to an older animal still—the stag. The stag leads them to one who is even older—the Owl of Cawlwyd. Gwrhyr speaks to the owl, saying, "We are King Arthur's messengers. We have come to you since we know of no animal older than you. What can you tell us of Mabon?" The owl replies, "I know nothing of Mabon, but I will be your guide and will lead you to an animal that God made before me." The owl then leads the party to the Eagle of Gwernaby, who in his turn leads them finally to the oldest animal of all—the salmon, who takes them to the castle where Mabon is imprisoned.

THE BIRD OF WISDOM

The owl is shown in this story as one of the five totem animals central to British tradition. Arthur's party encounters first the blackbird Druidh Dubh and then moves ever closer to the source of wisdom—the salmon. As a fish, the salmon swims in the River of Life, the Ocean of Being—his wisdom comes from an intimate participation in life. The owl imparts a different wisdom—one of objectivity and detachment. Like the figure of the Hermit in the Tarot, the owl watches and waits—in ruined castles, in church towers, in barns, in ivy bushes. Adept at disappearing from view and favoring the night, the owl is the animal that symbolizes esoteric wisdom and secrecy.

Because the owl is sacred to the Goddess in her crone-aspect, one of its many Gaelic names is *Cailleach-oidhche* (Crone of the Night). The barn owl is *Cailleach-oidhche gheal*, "white old woman of the night." The Cailleach is the goddess of death, and the owl's call was often sensed as an omen that someone would die. It was seen as a bird that calls for the soul, or that catches or takes it away. From Berne in Switzerland there comes a belief that the screech of an owl foretells either the birth of a child or the death of a man—pointing to the owl as a bird of the Goddess who is both taker and giver of life.

Knowing of an impending death or birth suggests that the owl is able to foretell the future, and the owl is indeed the totem bird of clairvoyance and astral travel. The veils which surround the normal boundaries of space and time can be pierced, if you take the owl as ally.

THE SECRET FAITH

In later times, all that was sacred to the Goddess and the "Secret Faith" was denigrated and labeled as evil by the Church in an attempt to convert people from their traditional ways. We see this process of denigration clearly in the folklore of the owl. Originally a sacred bird embodying wisdom and discernment, it gradually came to be seen only as a bird of ill-omen. Farmers would nail their bodies to barn doors or walls; the fern owl was named "Puck" or "Puck-bird"—an old word for the devil; and owls in general were called "constables from the dark land." It became a common saying that the owl was a transformation of one of the servants of the ten kings of hell.

The owl features strongly in the Welsh story from the *Mabinogion, Math, Son of Mathonwy*. Because it was written down from oral tradition in the twelfth or thirteenth century, it is hard to disentangle the pre-Christian from the Christian influences. Certainly in this tale the owl is considered an unfavorable bird. Arianrhod, the mother of Lleu Llaw Gyffes (the Bright One of the Skillful Hand), swears that Lleu will never take a human wife. But, eager for a companion, Lleu and the magician Gwydion fashion from the flowers of oak, broom, and meadowsweet, a woman called Blodeuwedd. A while later, Blodeuwedd falls in love with a hunter, and together they attempt to murder Lleu, who escapes in the form of an eagle. Gwydion eventually finds the eagle and, striking it with his wand, returns Lleu to human form. He then pursues Blodeuwedd, and rather than killing her, transforms her into an owl, saying: "And because of the dishonor thou hast done to Lleu Llaw Gyffes thou art never to dare show thy face in the light of day, and that through fear of all birds; and that there be enmity between thee and all birds, and that it be their nature to mob and molest thee wherever they may find thee; and that thou shalt not lose thy name, but that thou be for ever called Blodeuwedd."

The owl is a bird set apart. She stands on the threshold of the Otherworld, reminding us of the ever-present reality of death. But death is the great initiator and as the owl hoots to us from the trees we may come to realize in the depths of our being that our death in reality marks a beginning and not an end.

CAT
Cat

Guardianship, Detachment, Sensuality

The card shows a wild cat in the Scottish highlands. In the foreground we see the yellow-flowered spotted cat's ear and the pink flowering cat's foot. Hill-cat's glove (pennywort) is growing by the cat's tail.

Cat brings us the ability to observe situations quietly without judgement, before making decisions. Apparently asleep, but really listening, a cat can sit for hours until it acts with decisiveness. Remember the saying "A cat may look at a king." You have a right to know and to judge important issues for yourself in your own time.

The cat unites an awareness of the spirit-world with a highly developed sensuality. These two attributes are not polar opposites as dualistic spiritual teachings would have us believe, but are facets of one continuum of awareness and sensitivity. Working toward wholeness involves enhancing our appreciation of both the physical and non-physical worlds.

CAT

Drawn reversed, this card may mean that you must be wary of becoming an axen-cat, an old term which means a fireside cat, too lazy to bother much about the world. An indolent and self-absorbed sensuality, rather than an opening of the self to the magic of the physical world, is usually a means of escaping from reality. The cat is easily able to travel in her spirit-form in the Otherworld, but it is important for you to be strongly earthed in everyday physical reality. An interest in the mysterious and the occult can sometimes be inappropriate, especially if it is used as a defense against the pain and difficulty of being in the world.

The Tradition of the CAT

On Brighid's Day, the cats will bring home the brushwood
Traditional Scottish

The cat, whether wild or domestic, is sacred to the Goddess in Druid tradition, appearing in Irish, Welsh and Breton folklore. But it is in Scotland that we find a particularly powerful connection, and the wild cat can now only be found in the Highlands. A number of Scottish clans held the cat as their totem animal: those of MacIntosh, MacNeishe and MacNicol the domestic cat, and the MacBain the wild cat. The cat-people, a Pictish tribe known as the Kati, lived in Caithness, the ness or promontory of the cats, and Sutherland in Gaelic is *Cataobh*—cat country.

In Ireland, and almost certainly throughout the Celtic world, the skin of a wild cat was used by warriors. An ancient Irish bard speaks of Talc son of Trone, who is called the cat-headed chief, since his battle-dress included the skin of a wild cat, with its head attached to his helmet. The Irish *Yellow Book of Lecan* describes warriors wearing cats' heads, one of whom was noted as a Gaelic champion, and one of the Irish kings was called *Cairbar cinn chait*—Carbar of the cat's head.

THE CAT AS "UNHOLY"
Although the cat was used by warriors, as was the boar, raven and bear, to invoke the avenging and protective power of the gods, it

55

was still considered an animal associated with the Goddess and the feminine. For this reason we find both positive and negative attributes of the cat in folklore and tradition. As an animal clearly of the Goddess and in close contact with the spirit-world, the cat has been the victim of extraordinary persecution and cruelty. Her ability to see and work in the spirit-world makes the cat an ideal ally for any shaman or magician, and it was due to the Church's fear of such powers that many thousands of cats were tortured and put to death by burning in baskets in both Britain and France.

Roasting cats was not, unfortunately, confined to the Christian era. An ancient Celtic way of seeking information from cats, called *Taghairm*, was employed in Scotland, in which a live cat was tortured by roasting on a spit until other cats appeared to give the information which would save their colleague, or until the king of the *Cath Sith* (the fairy cats), Big Ears, would appear to give the answers. Since this practice has been reported in the Christian era, it is possible that it is apocryphal.

The cat as a creature of the Goddess was often perceived as somehow "unholy." A traditional saying in Ireland was "God save all here except the cat." It was considered unlucky to see a cat as the first animal of the year, unless you were a MacIntosh or of the clan Cattan (whose chieftain is called The Great Cat), and still today many people believe that a black cat crossing their path brings bad luck. But the cat is also the "pussy," a common term for the vulva, the place of origins, of the Goddess, of sensuality and mystery. Out of an oracular cave-shrine at Clough in Connaught, a "slender black cat reclining upon a chair of old silver" would give answers to those seeking advice, and three cats, described as "druidic beasts," emerged from the cave-mouth of Cruachan—the entrance to the Underworld.

"IT WAS BRIGHID'S CAT THAT EAT THE BACON"
Traditional Irish

The goddess Brighid, who is known in Irish tradition as "the daughter of the bear," had a cat as a companion. In Welsh tradition, we read of the cat in her fiercer role: the goddess Ceridwen in her manifestation as the great sow Henwen gives birth to a wolf-cub, an eagle, a bee and a kitten. Unfortunately this last grows into the Palug Cat—one of the Three Plagues of Anglesey—that is killed by King Arthur and Cai only after a lengthy struggle.

Another tale which shows the fierceness of the cat and its role as a guardian can be found in the Irish *Voyage of Maelduin*, one of four spiritual stories called *immrama*, meaning mystical voyages. In this tale, the druid Nuca teaches Maelduin how to build a magical boat, in which he plans to avenge the murder of his father. He and his companions almost reach the murderers' island, but winds blow them out to sea and they are lost for three days and nights. They then come to a series of islands, many of which are presided over by animals. The first is the Island of Giant Ants, the second the Island of Many Birds, and so on until they reach the tenth—the Island of the Cat. There they discover "a noble hall, a king's fit dwelling." Food and drink is in copious supply, and there are soft beds and golden benches for them to rest upon. In this great hall lies treasure: silver brooches, gold-hilted swords and wide necklets. But no one is present except a "quick hungry cat poised on a pillar." Against Maelduin's wishes, his foster-brother tries to steal a gold necklace, but in a moment his body is turned to a pile of ash by the "fiery paw of the wondrous cat." The cat is seen here in her role as guardian of Otherworldly treasure.

The cat teaches us respect and caution. She is sensual and will accept our affection but only on her terms. She is proud, in-dependent and capable of observing both this world and the next. Throughout Britain there have always been sightings of mysterious "big cats." Some believe they have escaped from zoos, others believe that every so often the *Cath Sith*, the cats of Faery, allow themselves to be glimpsed, to remind us of the existence of the Otherworld.

CRANE
Corr

CRANE

Secret Knowledge, Patience, Longevity

The card shows a crane fishing in a pool. Its legs are crossed to show the Ogham letter *Muinn*, and it gazes into the water, patiently waiting for sight of a fish. Behind the pool is a cave entrance to the Underworld, and in the evening sky the full moon is rising. In the foreground grow bitter vetch (*Cairmeal* from *Corr*) and bloody crane's bill.

Corr brings the qualities of patience and perseverance. The crane will stand for hours peering into the water until the time is right for it to dart at its prey. Combined with the ability to be patient, the crane conveys the capacity to be focused and to be able to concentrate without distraction. It brings an ability to guide others into the Underworld, to help them with their transition at the time of dying, or with their journeying in the inner realms. As well as conveying an ability to work in the "Underworld," the crane symbolizes arcane science, or Secret Knowledge, which in the Druid tradition is represented by the Ogham script—the tree-language of Druidry. In its widest sense, learning this language involves learning to read the "Book of Nature."

Drawn reversed: the crane stands alone for hours on end, simply observing and patiently waiting. But it is also able to join its colleagues to fly in formation or to dance together. You may need to learn the right balance between being alone and working with others. Spending too much time alone can create feelings of isolation and separation. Conversely, having no time to oneself can be an avoidance of self-knowledge and the uncomfortable feelings of loneliness. Spend a while looking at your life to see whether you give yourself enough time having both these experiences. The "shadow" side of the crane is manifested as harshness, meanness and a nagging, complaining disposition. If you find these qualities showing sometimes in your behavior, see if you can experience the deeper aspects of the crane, in which it becomes an animal of the Goddess-as-crone or wise-woman. Ask yourself to what extent you are denying the wise-woman who has a knowledge of death and the Underworld in yourself, and to what extent your negative behavior may be a reflection of this denial.

The Tradition of the CRANE

Comely Conaire slept on the side of Tara of the plains; when the cunning well-made man awoke, the crane-bag was found about his neck
From the Fionn cycle

On the island of Inis-Kea, off the coast of County Mayo, lives a lonely crane who has been there since the beginning of the world—and who will continue to live there until our world ends. This ancient bird is known in the Irish tales as "one of the wonders" and has come to symbolize longevity.

The crane, or heron, is one of the four most frequently-mentioned birds of the ancient Irish and British tradition—the others being the raven, swan and eagle. Since it was a sacred bird, to eat crane's flesh was taboo, although later this reverence was set aside and it became a delicacy. The crane was said to be one of the first birds to greet the sunrise, and was accorded the ability to predict rains and storms.

THE TREE ALPHABET

The association of the crane with knowledge comes not only from its link with the sunrise and therefore the East, the place of knowledge, but also from its association with Ogham, the tree alphabet of the Druids. Ogham was given to humanity by Ogma Sun Face, who purposely intended it for the use only of the learned. Later, when further Ogham glyphs were added, Greek mythographers credited Palamedes with their invention, saying he received his inspiration from observing a flock of cranes "which make letters as they fly." Since it was known only to the Druids, the term "Crane Knowledge" came to be used to denote knowledge of the Ogham in particular, and of arcane science in general. As Druidry gave way to Christianity, the term "Crane Cleric" came to be used to signify a high level of wisdom in certain priests, such as St. Columba of Iona.

An early Irish text tells us how the sea-god Manannan possessed a bag made from the skin of a crane. In this crane-bag he carried his own shirt, a strip from a whale's back, the King of Scotland's shears, the King of Lochlain's helmet, the bones of Assail's swine and Goibne's smith-hook. Some say that the crane-bag became the Druid's medicine-bag, in which he carried his Koelbren lots—carved Ogham-sticks used for divination. The crane-bag is a powerful symbol of the womb or fetal sac, and this symbolism is deepened when we learn that the Crane was considered a bird of the Goddess. Cranes often appear in threes. In the Irish *Book of Leinster*, a god of the Tuatha De Danann, the divine Midhir, has three cranes guarding his castle. They had the magical ability to rob any attacker of the will to fight. Three cranes protect the entrances to *Annwn*, the Underworld; three cranes stand on a bull's back in Gaulish carvings. All these cranes probably symbolize the triple-aspected Goddess: the Three Muses, the Three Fates, the Sisters of Wyrd.

GRANDMOTHER CRANE

The association of the crane with the bull is reinforced when we read in the Irish tale "The Hag of the Temple" that the hag's four sons have been turned into cranes who can only become human if the blood of an enchanted bull is sprinkled over them. In other stories the crane is a symbol of the dark aspect of the Goddess, and, like the raven, it becomes a bird to be feared as a harbinger of death or bad luck. With its harsh and raucous cry, it came to typify the nagging, scolding hag and to be associated with mean and unpleasant women. Here the association is with the Cailleach, the crone or hag, but a more positive representation of this aspect of the Goddess is depicted in the Irish tale which tells of Fionn falling over a cliff when a child. His grandmother saves him by turning into a crane and breaking his fall.

As a bird of the Cailleach, the crane is a bird of old age, and hence longevity, and is also a psychopomp—a guide in the Underworld after death. This symbolism is found both in the West and the East: cranes are shown on church carvings sucking the spirit from dying people to carry it safely away, and in China the soul of the dead was represented as riding on the crane's back to the "Western Heaven"—in the Celtic and Druid tradition the soul would be taken to the "Isles in the West."

Cranes dance in circles: and the ancients associated this ring dance both with the movement of the sun and with the cranes' role as Underworld guides, leading souls out of incarnation and back again to birth (in their variant the stork). Ritual crane dances were known in China, Siberia and Greece, and may well have been enacted by Druid shamans too—using, significantly, nine steps and a leap as a basic theme, and weaving in and out of a maze or labyrinthine pattern to symbolize the journey of the soul.

FROG
Losgann

FROG

Sensitivity, Medicine, Hidden Beauty and Power

The card shows a common frog crawling from a pool in which lies frogspawn, traditionally considered a powerful medicine. To the right grows *muileag*—frogberry, now known as cranberry, and frog's spindle or orchid. To the left beneath the hanging willow leaves grow toadstool mushrooms, which were once called frogstools.

Losgann unites the elements of water and earth, bringing joy, delight and healing in its singing and hopping, and leading you to the sacred spring from which you may be refreshed and renewed. A cold-blooded creature living half on the land and half in the water, the frog possesses an extremely sensitive skin, considered magical by shamans. A companion of the rain spirits, the frog can help you develop your sensitivity to others, to healing and to sound through your skin and your whole body and aura.

Nothing is what it appears to be, and life is more fun than you at first supposed! There is a hidden beauty and a hidden power in all of nature, and as you open yourself to this you will feel close to the Goddess and close to both the earth and to water. Look for the beauty and the magic **behind** appearances.

Drawn reversed, this card suggests that you are learning how to embrace difficult circumstances. The frog that you must marry may well turn out to be a prince. The circumstances you have chosen to accept—whilst apparently unappealing or difficult— may well bring you rich rewards in the end. Remember that the frog brings medicine, and medicine brings healing.

The Tradition of the FROG

'Tis not where water is a frog will be, but where a frog is water will be
Traditional

Water was considered sacred by the Druids, and every river, spring, and well had its guardian spirit or deity. Votive offerings of wood, silver, gold, and bronze were made to the spirits of rivers and lakes, to such a degree that the Romans would auction the contents of lakes in Celtic areas to speculators before they had conquered the territory surrounding them. Both frogs and their close relatives toads are found at water sources. As animals that are seeded in pools, and which frequent them when grown, they were sometimes considered as representatives of the water-spirits. In Acton Barnett in Shropshire, by an ancient healing spring, it was said that the spirits of the well would appear as three frogs. The largest of the three was always to be addressed as the Dark God. His darkness is related to the fact that both frog and toad were seen as creatures in contact with the Underworld. For this reason, in the popular imagination they became associated with witchcraft and potion-brewing—the toad or frog was often the witch's familiar who would croak warnings of danger to its mistress, and the toad was reputed to be a common ingredient in witches' brews.

Both these associations point to deeper truths. As familiar of the witch or Ovate (the Druid equivalent as healer and seer), the frog is an ally who brings the blessings of the water spirits—the healing blessings of rain and purification. The frog also brings its own medicine and was seen as a healing messenger of the Mother Goddess. Its ashes were supposed to prevent haemorrhaging; its spawn was considered a cure for rheumatism and inflammatory diseases. Sore eyes could be cured if someone would agree to lick the eye of a frog and then the sore eye.

Far from being considered a poisonous ingredient of brews, we can see that the frog and toad were medicine in the old days—bringing healing in a subtle way through their connection with the water sprites, and in a tangible way through their physical properties.

Their connection with the Mother Goddess can also be traced to the tradition which states that it is lucky to have a frog living in a dairy—it guards the milk churn—and milk is naturally associated with the Goddess. A further connection with milk is found in an image of the Celtic goddess Luxuria depicted with a fox between her legs and a toad hanging from each breast.

THE FROG PRINCE

The frog-as-aristocrat is a theme that runs through storytelling from the earliest days up to present times with the inimitable Toad of Toad Hall in *The Wind in the Willows*. In the earlier tales, the frog or toad was in reality a prince. From the Western Isles of Scotland comes a tale of a queen who was ill and could only be healed by a drink from "the well of true water." Each of the queen's three daughters was sent to fetch the drink, but, each time, a hideous *losgann* appeared and denied them access to the well unless they agreed to marry him. The youngest daughter agreed, and was able to heal her mother. But that night, the frog came to her door calling: "Gentle one, gentle one, rememberest thou the little pledge thou gavest me beside the well, my love, my love." The girl let him in, put him by the door, and went back to bed. But he repeated his call until she was obliged to put him under a mug to silence him. Still he called, so she made him a bed by the fireside. His cries continued, so she moved his bed beside hers. Although he continued to plead, she ignored him until finally he said, "You'd better put an end to my torture and chop off my head!" As soon as she struck him, he turned into a handsome young man, married the princess, and eventually became king.

From Brittany comes a similar tale—containing the essential components of the frog being associated with a well or spring, the youngest daughter agreeing to marry the hideous creature, and it turning out to be a handsome prince. Both tales demonstrate the rich rewards that await those who are able to make a sacrifice out of a desire to heal and devotion to a loved one. Both tales also re-inforce the connection between the frog and the Goddess telling of the healing of a mother-queen and of her three daughters.

THE STONE OF POWER

The frog or toad carrying a secret within is the possessor of a power object—a dark gray or light brown stone said to be found in the heads of very old specimens. This mythological object has been known by many names, including Crepandia, Borax, Stelon, and Bufonite. The frog or toad, adder, otter, and fox are all carriers of these secret, invisible power objects. The otter and fox carry magical pearls, the adder leaves a serpent's stone, and the toad or frog when old carries the stone of magical properties in its head. These objects, at one level, represent a crossing-over from the animal to the mineral realm—rendering the transient life of the animal eternally cast within a stone. By carrying such a stone, and using it magically, the Druid or shaman would be able to contact his ally, the animal spirit.

RAVEN
Bran

RAVEN

Healing, Initiation, Protection

The card shows a raven perched on the bare winter branches of a beech tree that grows beside an ancient mound. This is the White Mount, in which is buried the head of Bran the Blessed, and on which in later times will be raised the Tower of London.

Bran offers initiation, protection and the gift of prophecy. What is meant by initiation in practice may be as formal as actually undergoing an initiation ceremony, or as informal as, for example, being initiated into the mysteries of a new post or profession. It marks the death of one thing, which gives way to the birth of another. The power of the raven can also bring you the very deepest form of healing, which is achieved through a process known as "the resolution of the opposites"—giving you the possibility of resolving conflicts that have long lain buried in your unconscious or perhaps in your past.

Drawn reversed, this card suggests that you should become aware of the forces of destruction that exist in your life and in the world. However much we might wish that destruction did not occur, we know that without destruction there cannot be construction and re-creation. The raven speaks of the knowledge of the dark and difficult aspects of life, which it is hard for us to understand. Sometimes we, or our lives, must go through a process of disintegration and darkness, in order to emerge into the greater light of a new morning. To a great extent our fear of the dark is worse than whatever it is that we find there. Drawing this card reversed may mean that we can now come to terms with our own destructiveness—a rage that has perhaps been buried for years—knowing that we have the protection of the Goddess. Deeper still, it may mean that we can come to a resolution of the conflict of opposites—experiencing the reality that in darkness there is light, and in light darkness.

The Tradition of the RAVEN

I have fled in the shape of a raven of prophetic speech
Taliesin

During the Second World War, the Tower of London was bombed. The ravens which had lived there for centuries flew away. Winston Churchill, who had been initiated into a Druid Order in 1908, immediately ordered their replacement with young ravens brought from north Wales and the wilds of northwest Scotland. But a first reading of the old tales that mention the raven suggest that it is a bird of ill-omen—bringing the fear of war, death and destruction. To understand Churchill's reasoning, we must turn to the tale of Bran the Blessed, in which the superhuman Bran (whose name means "Raven" or "Crow") asks that his head be cut off and buried on the White Mount in London, facing the direction of France. As long as the head remained buried it would protect the kingdom. The Tower of London was later raised on the site of the White Mount, and the totem power was transferred from the buried raven-god's head to the presence of actual ravens in the Tower to ensure the kingdom's safety.

Not only Caer Llundain, London, but also Lyons in France had the raven as its totem bird, and both cities were dedicated to the god Lugh, or Lud, who himself is associated with ravens. This god of Light was warned of the approach of his enemies, the Fomorians, by ravens before the second battle of Magh Tuiredh. The Old English epic *Beowulf* portrays the raven as the morning bird of joy and light, having helped Beowulf to victory. There is also a tradition that Arthur became a raven after his death, and in Somerset it was the custom to doff your hat to a raven as a mark of respect, for this very reason.

Churchill was clearly aware of the importance of the raven as one of the primary totem beasts of Britain. He must have known that ravens are sacred birds whose presence invokes protection. They will warn the forces of light of impending attack—as they did Beowulf and Lugh. And they will also strike fear into the hearts of the enemy. For this reason the Celts used the image of the raven on their armor—the most striking example of which is a battle-helmet found in Romania, surmounted by a large figure of a raven with hinged wings. As the warrior rushed forward, the wings would have flapped, striking terror into his foe—or at the least distracting him at a vital moment.

"VERY BLACK IS THE RAVEN, QUICK THE ARROW FROM THE BOW" *Triads*

Although the Irish war-goddesses the Badbh and the Morrigan are said to have often appeared on battlefields as ravens—causing fear and havoc among the warriors—a more accurate translation of the name of their totem bird is the hooded or scald-crow. This bird, and its close relative the raven, are scavengers who would certainly have been attracted to battlefields, and the message of their presence before the confronting armies would have been that in war no one wins except death itself.

As the bird of the Goddess in her death aspect, the crow or raven symbolizes the forces of destruction, of katabolism, which are as necessary to the continuation of life as the forces of creation and anabolism. Because of our fear of death and bloodshed, and because of the conflation of the two birds, the folklore and traditions surrounding the raven portray an ambiguous relationship to this natural but painful aspect of life. There is evidence that the fear and rejection of the raven are related not only to its association with death, but also to its association with the Goddess. Raven-women appear throughout Celtic and Arthurian literature, and the "raven knowledge" of the Druids was clearly a gift of the Goddess given to the Ovates, or Druid seers, which entailed an ability to see into the future and the past, and beyond the veil of death.

The raven as a bird of death or the Underworld was clearly recognized by the burying of ravens with wings outspread at the bottom of pits—such as at Danebury in Hampshire. These ritual pits or shafts symbolized the connection between this world and the Underworld, and the raven was a messenger between the two.

THE RAVEN AS A BIRD OF HEALING

By being able to travel from this world to the next, the raven symbolizes also the power of healing—but the type of healing that comes about through a radical confrontation with the unconscious, with the hidden, with the Shadow, and with the darker, potentially destructive aspects of the psyche. The raven's association with death becomes an association with depth and thus with depth psychology and the transformative powers of initiation—for such a moment marks to a greater or lesser extent the death of the old self, and the rebirth of a new self.

This therapeutic association of the raven explains the occurrence of raven images at some of the Celtic healing sanctuaries, and on Romano-Celtic iconography depicting beneficent divinities.

The raven's connection with healing is reinforced when we consider it as a bird of prophecy and divination, integral facets of the healer's art. The raven could travel to the darkest regions of the Underworld to bring back visions and oracular instructions for the seeker and healer.

The raven has been seen as an oracle for thousands of years. The early Irish Druids divined according to their flight and cries, and as late as 1694 it was reported that a Herefordshire raven uttered a prophecy three times.

SWAN
Eala

Soul, Love, Beauty

T he card depicts a scene from the Irish tale the *Dream of Oenghus*. In the foreground is the lake where a beautiful girl, Caer Ibormeith (Yewberry), changes into a swan every other year at the time of Samhuinn. To win her, Oenghus, the god of love, becomes a swan, and they both fly to his house, Brugh na Boinne — now known as Newgrange and pictured on the horizon. As with many swans that appear in the old tales, there is a gold chain around Yewberry's neck.

Eala brings us the qualities of soul — of love and depth, grace and beauty. Being associated with the Druid festival time of Samhuinn, the swan is also a bird of the threshold, and represents that part of us which can travel into the Otherworld. Drawing this card may indicate that you will receive inspiration from the Otherworld, or that love is entering into your life. It is auspicious to draw this card if you are preparing to write a song or poem, for the swan's skin and feathers were used to make the bard's ceremonial cloak, the *tugen*.

Drawn reversed, this card may mean that you need to come to terms with a separation. The old tales of the swan show that in reality there is no separation from the ones we love—only transformation from one form to another. But to continue our journey in this world, we need to be able to say "goodbye" to those we are separated from, even though we know that ultimately we may be together again. The separation we are faced with, however, may be internal rather than external, and Eala may be calling us to connect more deeply with our own soul.

The Tradition of the SWAN

White Swans of the Wilderness, ye have flown over many lands. Tell me, have ye seen aught of Tir-na n'Og, where no one loses youth; or Tir-na-Moe, where all that is beautiful lives for ever; or Moy-Mell, that is so honey-sweet with blossom?
From "The Children of Lir" retold by Ella Young

Tir-na n'Og was the name of the Land of Eternal Youth in the Otherworld. The White Swans of the Wilderness were four children of the Tuatha De Danaan, one of the earliest races to inhabit Ireland, having originally come from the northern Greek isles. They became the faery folk—the *Sidhe*—who lived underground, in the Hollow Hills, when they were driven there by the invasion of the Milesians. Although the Danaans were a mythological race, history and myth have become inextricably entwined, and there are indeed traces of trade and travel between the lands of ancient Greece and the British Isles. This may explain the use of Pythagorean mathematics in the construction of the old stone circles, and the many similarities in Greek and Celtic mythology and philosophy.

In Greek mythology, the swan was Apollo's bird and was often pictured singing to the lyre. Its association with grace, beauty and the feminine has been so strong that it has also been associated with song in the Celtic tradition. We talk still of a "swan-song"—the last performance, work of art, or gesture made shortly before a person dies. Such an act is possibly called a swan-song because the swan represents the human soul in the Otherworld. The swan is one of the four most frequently mentioned birds in the old tales—along with the raven, crane and eagle. Whereas the crane is often pictured carrying the soul to the Otherworld, the swan depicts the soul itself. For this reason, the swan is often associated with the time of Samhuinn, the gateway between the realm of the living and that of the dead—the inner and outer worlds—the old and new years. To a lesser extent, the gateway of Midsummer Eve, during which time it is easier to contact the faery realm, is also associated with the swan through the European tales of maidens who turn into swans at this time.

THE SWANS OF LIR

In Ireland in the old days, if you saw a swan you would say, "My blessing with you, white swan, for the sake of Lir's children!" Lir was a king of the Tuatha De Danaan, who had four beautiful children—three sons and a daughter. They were loved by all, except their stepmother Aoifa, who hated them. As they were bathing, she struck each of them with a druidic wand and turned them into four white swans. She told them they would remain as swans for nine hundred years until they heard a bell tolling and the news that a prince from the north would marry a princess from the south. They were still able to speak and sing as humans, though, and their desolate father, Lir, came to the shore of the lake to beg them to come home with him, but·Conn—one of his sons—told him: "May good fortune be on the threshold of your door from this time and for ever, but we cannot cross it, for we have the hearts of wild swans and we must fly in the dusk and feel the water moving under our bodies; we must hear the lonesome cries of the night. We have the voices only of the children you knew; we have the songs you taught us—that is all. Gold crowns are red in the firelight, but redder and fairer is dawn."

Nine hundred years passed, by which time Ireland had become Christian. The swans heard the bells of St. Kernoc's church and came to the Saint, who took care of them. Soon after, a princess of

Munster married King Largnen of Connacht, and the four children of Lir were released from Aoifa's spell. But as their swan skins fell from them, they became humans nine hundred years old and immediately died of old age. St. Kernoc buried them together in an earth mound, with a tombstone bearing their names in Ogham.

SWAN MAIDENS

The *Dream of Oenghus* also tells of humans who become swans—151 women, each wearing a silver chain (except Yewberry, the tallest and wearing a gold chain), who on alternate Samhuinns gather at a lake to transform themselves into swans. The love-god Oenghus on seeing Yewberry calls her to him, promising to return with her into the lake. He puts his arms around her and makes love to her in the form of a swan. They then fly together to Newgrange, having first circled the lake three times, lulling everyone to sleep for three days and three nights with their ethereal song.

The Ulster demi-god Cu-Chulainn is strongly associated with swans; a flock of them appeared at his conception, and reappear frequently throughout his adulthood. One Samhuinn his chariot gets stuck in a marsh, and he frees it with their help. In another story, he is pursued by two women who become swans the more effectively to chase him.

The swan's graceful form clearly connects it to the Goddess, and to the qualities of beauty and femininity, which is why the theme of maidens turned into swans occurs in folk-tales throughout the world—the most well-known being enacted in the ballet *Swan Lake*. But the theme of the maiden turning into a swan is also an allegory of death—the swan representing the soul, which is usually seen as feminine.

WOLF
Faol

WOLF

Intuition, Learning,
The Shadow

The card shows a wolf stalking in the forest near the source of the river Findhorn in Scotland. The last wolf in Britain was killed here in 1743. It is the time of *Faoilleach* — the Wolf-month, the last fortnight of winter and the first of spring, generally corresponding to February. In the foreground we see snowdrops, the flower of the Druid festival of Imbolc at the beginning of February.

Faol brings a strong sense of faithfulness, inner strength and intuition. But the wolf brings learning too. Sometimes you need to cross barriers, to take risks, to go beyond the limited compass of "normal" behavior in order to learn and grow, although crossing these boundaries may seem unattractive, even painful. You need not fear the inner power and strength you feel when you spend time alone. Come to know your deepest self and even in the darkest places you will find courage and spiritual companionship.

Drawn reversed, this card may suggest that you need to come into a new relationship with your sense of aloneness in the world. Behind a fear of loneliness may lie a fear of your own inner strength, fierceness and power. Learn to trust this and to come to know your deeper self. Through dreams and intuitions you may come to learn more of the hidden side of your being which is sometimes called the Shadow. As well as there being "lone wolves" in the world, you should know that the wolf is a faithful animal which often mates for life. In tradition, it was considered lucky when a wolf crossed the path of a bridal party, precisely because of this faithfulness. Even though you may need to spend times of your life alone, you should know that you will also have times of companionship and togetherness.

The Tradition of the WOLF

The sign-bearing wolf shall lead his troops, and surround
Cornwall with his tail
The Prophecies of Merlin

The wolf is a powerful totem animal, embodying many of the qualities of the hound, but including a wildness not found in the domesticated dog. One of the Gaelic names for the wolf is *Madadh-Allaidh*, the wild dog, and the Celts were known for their cross-breeding of wolves with hounds to produce a powerful fighting dog for battle.

In Ireland there is a "Fort of the Wolves" and a legend which tells of a struggle between the hero Cu-Chulainn and the war-goddess the Morrigan, in which the hero, for daring to spurn her amorous advances, is attacked by the goddess who has taken the form of a she-wolf.

But despite these associations with fierceness, the wolf was valued more for its affinities with humans than for its wildness. In reality, the wolf is a highly social, intelligent and friendly animal. Fondness for the wolf in Celtic tradition is shown in the legend that as a baby King Cormac of Ireland was taken by a she-wolf while his mother lay sleeping. Reared with the cubs, he always had a soft spot for wolves, and even when he was made king a pack of wolves accompanied him wherever he went. One of the gifts to Wales of the goddess Ceridwen in her guise as Henwen, the great white sow, was a wolf-cub, and in Geoffrey of Monmouth's *The Life of Merlin*, we read of Merlin finding companionship in a dying wolf during his time of madness in the forest. As winter begins, depriving him of food, Merlin turns to his animal-friend: "You, O wolf, dear companion, accustomed to roam with me through the secluded paths of the woods and meadows, now can scarcely get across the fields . . . You lived in these woods before I did and age has whitened your hairs first."

THE WOLF AS CLAN TOTEM

In Scottish tradition a number of clans have the wolf as their totem: the MacLennans and Mac Tyres (both meaning Son of the Wolf) and the MacMillans (meaning Son of the Wolf Servant); the personal name Fillan comes from the Gaelic *Faolan*, little wolf. In Wales, names such as Bledyn, Bleddri and Bleiddudd all derive from the word for wolf—*Blaidd*. In Ireland one whole tribe claimed descent from a wolf, and according to tradition wolves were tamed and adopted as godfathers and godmothers.

In the late Iron Age wolves were favorite subjects in iconography, and in the high mountain sanctuary of Le Donon in the Vosges there is a sculpture of a hunter-god and forest benefactor who wears a wolfskin cape. The Celts used the pelts of wolves as rugs and sat on them while dining, and there was a folk-belief that the hide offered protection from epilepsy. Wolf teeth were considered especially lucky—they were rubbed on babies' gums when teething, and were worn as charms and ornaments.

A wolf is one of the animal allies of the horned figure on the great Celtic cauldron found at Gundestrup in Denmark. The others are a stag, a snake, a boar, two bulls, two lions and a dolphin.

THE WEREWOLF

Despite all the positive associations with the wolf in tradition, it has also come to represent danger and to evoke fear. In Anglo-Saxon times wolves were sometimes hung beside criminals, who were themselves termed wolves, and the Saxon word for gallows means "wolf-tree." Ever since the first century AD there have been tales of werewolves—humans who transform themselves into wolves. These stories probably arose from a variety of causes, and the many people who were burned alive as werewolves during the sixteenth century, mostly in France, probably included sufferers from porphyria, a genetic disease resulting in an aversion to daylight and the growth of facial hair, sufferers from rabies contracted through wolf-bites, and people showing symptoms of ergot poisoning, besides the truly criminal such as child or mass murderers. Certainly tales of the predations of hungry wolves on livestock and perhaps humans, combined with the perceived dangers of attacks from rabid wolves, made the wolf a hated and feared animal in post-Celtic Europe. The lone and potentially murderous wolf became a symbol for all that was to be rejected and loathed—including man's own darkest urges.

Despite the strongly negative associations of the wolf over the last two millennia, typified in the stories of Little Red Riding Hood, the Big Bad Wolf and other European folk-tales, sufficient connection with the true nature of the wolf and its ancestral totemic and positive associations existed for Baden-Powell, when founding the Boy Scout movement, to ask children to call themselves wolf-cubs, and for the cub-leader to be called Akela, the wolf-pack leader of Rudyard Kipling's *Jungle Book*. Some naturalists believe that wolves use ravens to guide them to sources of food, and certainly ravens will often follow wolves. There is a powerful connection between wolf and raven at the totemic level also.

Just as Merlin found companionship in a wolf, so can we, if Faol becomes our ally, find closeness and spiritual companionship with this most faithful of animal guides. Above all, Faol will teach us, through our experience, to trust ourselves and not to fear or reject those parts of us that we do not yet understand or know.

ADDER
Nathair

ADDER

Transformation,
Healing, Life Energy

The card depicts a pair of adders. Druids were sometimes called Adders, and it is possible that the story of St. Patrick ridding Ireland of snakes refers to the Druids. In the background we see the Druid snake-stone altar in Cumbria, covered in ivy—a plant which, like the snake, is poisonous and yet which also speaks of the mystery of death and rebirth, and of the soul's journey through the labyrinth from this world to the next and back again. We see such a labyrinth symbolically depicted in the maze carved on the rock face. Such patterns have been found in many places, including Tintagel in Cornwall. In the foreground are ammonite and sea urchin fossils—both of which may have been used by Druids as magical "adder stones."

Nathair offers healing and transformation. Its ability to glide into the darkness through crevices in the rocks connects it to the Under or Otherworld, and the realm of Death. It is the totem animal of the Earth Goddess, and also the Sky Father Sun God, and represents our ability to die and be reborn. The energy that enables us to be born on earth is sexual energy, but this also necessitates our death. Befriending adder or snake power will enable you to journey through life gracefully and magically, shedding your old life easily when the time comes—whether that old life be of the physical body or of a stage in this present incarnation.

Drawn reversed, this card urges you to abandon the ability to wound and to replace it with the power to heal. Although the snake is poisonous, and has been used in the Christian tradition as a symbol of evil, in the Druid and other traditions it represents healing and the power of transformation. The snake as totem animal urges us to use our powers of energy, penetration, swift and silent movement, not to harm others but, on the contrary, to help and heal them. We can learn how to love and channel the serpent currents which flow through our body and the body of the earth so that they become beneficent, healing, life-giving currents that ultimately flow—like the meandering snake-rivers of the plains—to the wide sea.

The Tradition of the ADDER

I am a Serpent, I am Love; I have been an Adder of the Mountain; I have been a Serpent in the River
Taliesin

Follow the adder through the grass. He invites you to become him as he glides into a tiny crack in the rock face. You find yourself entering a dark, moist world that is normally hidden from you. Down you go into the earth, and as you delve, you let go of all your worries and start to forget who you are, you lose track of time and it seems forever before you find yourself gliding toward a glimmer of light. As you approach this light, the crevice through which you must emerge is so narrow it presses your body on either side, and as you push your way through you find your skin is sloughing away. You emerge on to the grass with your new skin glistening in the brightness of the morning.

The snake's ability to shed its skin, suggesting that it holds the key to the mysteries of healing and rebirth, and its sinuous movement which echoes the movement of life-force through the body and earth-energy through the land, makes the snake a powerful and central symbol in the Druid tradition. The Welsh bards even referred to the Druids as *Naddred*—Adders.

THE SYMBOL OF FERTILITY

Ancient Druid altars, phallic in shape, have been found in Maryport in Cumbria and Lypiatt Park in Gloucestershire. The Cumbrian altar has a snake with an egg in its mouth carved on one side of the phallus, while the Gloucestershire altar depicts a snake wound around the central stone.

The snake with an egg in its mouth suggests that the ancients knew of the details of conception—with the snake being the sperm and the egg the ovum. That somehow, perhaps through clairvoyance, the Druids were aware of the mechanics of conception is further supported by images resembling sperm penetrating ova that appear in Pictish rock carvings in Scotland.

Although, as symbols of the penis or sperm, snakes could represent male sexuality, they were often associated with the Goddess as well as the God. They were guardians of wells sacred to the Goddess, and would accordingly curl up in them at night. They were sacred to Brighid, goddess of wells, water, and fire, and even when she became Christianized as St. Bride, the Gaelic hymns retained this connection:

> *Early on Bride's morn*
> *Shall the serpent come from the hole,*
> *I will not harm the serpent,*
> *Nor will the serpent harm me.*

The snake was a symbol of fertility—its shape and the fact that it has a double penis made it an obvious associate of fertility gods such as Cernunnos, who is often depicted holding snakes, or even with his legs formed by snakes. But the female snake represents fertility too, giving birth to a prodigious number of young, her sinuous movements echoed in the path of meandering rivers. The Cuckmere in Sussex, for example, was known as Snake River, and the river-goddess Verbeia of the Wharfe in Yorkshire was depicted holding a snake in each hand.

NWYVRE AND THE SNAKE-STONE

By representing the procreative ability of both genders, the snake was used to denote the mystery of both physical and metaphysical procreation. As potentially poisonous it acts as a guardian of the central mystery of the secret of regeneration through the proper direction of the life-force, the *Nwyvre*, as it is known in the Druid tradition—*Kundalini* in the Eastern tradition. The image of two snakes entwined represents the dual nature of this power which, when united, produces new life. In Wales there was a tradition that every farmhouse had two snakes, a male and a female, and that these ensured the well-being of the household. In Eastern imagery, *Kundalini* is sometimes represented as two snakes, Ida and Pingala. In the West we have the image of the Caduceus of Mercury—used to represent the healing profession—suggesting that true healing can only come about through the wholeness represented by the union of the two snakes. In the Druid tradition, the symbol of this union, the serpent's egg, was of central importance.

This egg is one of the most treasured possessions of a Druid. With many magical properties, it is known in Welsh as the *glain neidre*—adder stone—or *gleini na Droedh*—the Druid's gem. Some say it was a talisman made of glass, and it is possible that the Druid alchemists, the Pheryllt, were also glass-makers. Others say it may have been a fossilized ammonite or sea urchin, or the shiny egg-case of the whelk which is sometimes washed ashore. If earth energy is seen as serpentine, then fossils could be treasured as the "eggs" of these magical snakes. But however the Druid's adder stone is conceived materially, its true power lies in the inner realm, where it acts as a focus for the incubation and regeneration of the Self.

EAGLE
Iolair

EAGLE

Intelligence, Renewal, Courage

The card shows a golden eagle flying in front of the rising sun, indicating its association with the East—the realm of intellect and the element Air. It is the time of Lughnasadh (Lammas on August 1st)—and the landscape below shows the harvest being gathered in. On the horizon are the peaks of Snowdonia, and we can just make out the eagles' secret lake of renewal in the north. In the foreground is the oak tree, for the oak is king of the forest, as the eagle is king of the birds. The oak and the eagle are both also associated with the god Taranis, the Druid Jupiter, and the god Lugh, Lleu, who was said to have transformed himself into an eagle which perched on a mighty oak.

Iolair helps you to see your life in the wider context, enabling you to make decisions and chart your goals with clarity and objectivity. A powerful ally, it is courageous and strong, and draws its power from the sun. If you will allow the eagle to work for you, it will bring you a sense of purpose and the courage to see this through, enabling you to venture into fresh territory with confidence. It will allow you to detach yourself from everyday worries and cares, and will enable you to grasp subtle concepts. The eagle, when accepted, will also show you the way to renew and rejuvenate yourself, by demonstrating the art of plunging—at just the right moment—into the lake of the heart.

Drawn reversed, this card may mean that you need to guard against the dangers of an overpowering intellect. The eagle, when it knows how to renew itself in the secret lake, is able to balance its masculine fiery qualities with the feminine, watery qualities of the lake. But when it cannot find the secret lake, when we deny our minds access to the heart, our lives can become dry and sterile, our intellects harsh and overly analytical. Now may be the time to see whether your mind and heart are in balance. You may want to pay more attention to your dreams—to listen to the call of the unconscious, to the depths within, without denying the value of your questing, rational mind.

The Tradition of the EAGLE

I am an eagle on a rock
The Song of Amergin

High in the mountains of Snowdonia in Wales lies the secret burial-place of King Arthur. No one will ever be able to violate it, because it is guarded by two great eagles. These eagles are in reality two Druids who as shape-shifters have transformed themselves into eagles on constant patrol in the mountain wilderness. There is a Welsh saying, "the eagles are creating whirlwinds on Snowdon," which may well relate to the weather magic woven by the Druids on that sacred mountain. Their ability to shape-shift into eagles was recognized by the Scots, as well as the Welsh. It is said that three score Druids gathered as eagles each year at Beltane on an island in Loch Lomond to augur the omens for the coming year.

In Gaelic the eagle was sometimes called *Suil-na-Greine*, Eye of the Sun. This depiction of the eagle as a solar bird is found also in North America. The psychologist Carl Jung noted that the native American Indian "takes on something of the sun-like nature of this bird when he adorns himself with its feathers . . . the feather crest is a crown which is equivalent to the rays of the sun."

The kings of Ireland and Scotland wore plumes of eagle's feathers, and the Scottish clan chiefs wore three eagle plumes in their bonnets—reminiscent of the Druidic symbol *Awen*, or three bars of solar light.

REJUVENATION AND RENEWAL

There is an Irish tradition that Adam and Eve still exist as eagles, living at Bo-fin in Killery Bay, Galway. And an earlier Irish source, *The Voyage of Maelduin*, recounts how Maelduin and his companions watch an eagle rejuvenating itself in a secret lake. This theme of renewal is found also in the Bible, in Spenser's *Faerie Queene* and the reported writings of Albertus Magnus. Symbolically the eagle represents the intellect, the Super-ego, the conscious self, the heights. The lake represents the emotions, the unconscious, the depths. To find renewal, spiritual and psychological refreshment, and rejuvenation, we must periodically allow our intellects, our rational selves, the opportunity to plunge into the depths of feeling and the subconscious. In this way knowledge is transformed into wisdom.

THE EAGLE AND THE SALMON

The eagle is one of the four most frequently-mentioned birds of the ancient Irish and British tradition—the others being the raven, swan and crane. Eagles are particularly prominent in the Welsh tales. In *Culhwch and Olwen*, the earliest of stories to speak of King Arthur, we learn that the eagle is one of the five oldest animals in the world. To win Olwen's hand in marriage, Culhwch, together with a band of Arthur's men, struggles to complete thirty-nine tasks set by Olwen's father—the giant Yspadadden Pencawr. One of the tasks is to free Mabon, the Celtic Divine Youth or Son of Light. To do this they must seek the oldest animal in the world.

They visit an ancient blackbird, who directs them to the Stag of Rhedynfr, who in his turn directs them to the Owl of Cawlwyd, who leads them to the Eagle of Gwernaby. It is this great and ancient eagle, one of the primary totem beasts of Britain, who leads them finally to the oldest animal of all—the salmon, who takes them to the castle where Mabon is imprisoned.

The eagle and the salmon are deeply related at a symbolic level. The salmon, like the lake, represents the watery depths of emotion and the unconscious. The eagle catching the salmon can therefore represent the union of heights and depths, of intellect and emotion. The Pictish symbol of the fish eagle, found carved on ancient stones in Scotland, may be touching on the importance of this symbolism.

Math Son of Mathonwy, another tale in the Welsh collection of the *Mabinogion*, recounts how the supernatural being Lleu Llaw Gyffes has a curse put on him by his mother, to prevent him taking an earthly wife. But Lleu's uncle Math and Gwydion, a magician, conjure a wife for him—a woman of flowers called Blodeuwedd. She, however, is unfaithful and with her lover tries to murder Lleu. As he is run through with a spear, Lleu gives a great cry and turns into an eagle, which flies up into an oak tree. Later, Gwydion discovers the eagle, and striking him with his magic wand, returns Lleu to human form. Lleu Llaw Gyffes (the Bright One of the Skillful Hand) is the Welsh variant of the Irish solar god Lugh and in this story we see again the eagle's association with the sun, and with the Druid festival time of Lughnasadh.

SOW
Muc

**Generosity,
Nourishment, Discovery**

The card shows a sow with her piglets. In the fields behind her we see wheat and barley, said to have been brought to Wales by the divine sow Henwen, the "White Ancient." On the horizon we see the Hill of Tara, in Ireland, which was once known as Muc Inis, Pig Island, when the Tuatha De Danann changed it into the shape of a pig. In the foreground to the right grows sow-thistle, and to the left deadly nightshade, which—it is said—pigs can eat without harm. On the ground lies one of the favorite foods of pigs, the nuts of the beech tree.

Muc, with her large litters, symbolizes abundance and fertility. Drawn upright, this card may mean that you are called upon to be generous. Feeling connected to the love of the Goddess for all her creatures, you able to give freely, knowing that you, in turn, are nourished and sustained by her. Choosing this card, you can open yourself to the abundance that exists throughout nature. You can allow yourself to accept this abundance, knowing that life perpetually renews itself, and that you need not worry about ever being disconnected from it. Allow yourself to feast on life—to enjoy its beauties and its sensual delights. The Goddess is generous, giving to all and renewing all.

Drawn reversed, this card indicates that you may need to revise your image of yourself. There is an old saying in Gaelic: "When you thought you were on the sow's back, you were beside her in the puddle." Although the sow symbolizes nourishment, fertility and giving, she can also represent greed and "pig-ignorance." You may need to work toward a greater understanding of the subtleties of life, rather than relying simply on your looks or physique. Without wisdom even beauty can be unattractive, as another Gaelic saying indicates: "As a golden jewel in a pig's snout, is a fair woman without sufficiency of understanding." Pigs' bristles were used for centuries for artists' brushes, and the leather of pigs is exceptionally soft—appearances can be deceptive, so judge people or propositions on their true merits and intrinsic worth rather than their outward appearance.

The Tradition of the SOW

The pig that I killed last year
Has produced young this year
Traditional riddle

Much of the ancient wisdom has entered our everyday world through traditional sayings. Riddles, particularly, were used by the Bards to convey ideas with humor and to test the wits of their audience. The riddle of the pig that produces young, even though killed, refers to a coppiced tree—which appears to have been cut down, until its new shoots are seen in the spring. But beneath this straightforward answer lies a clue that directs us to the symbolic and totemic meaning of the pig in the Druid tradition. The pig is sacred to the Goddess, the providing and nourishing aspect of .

divinity, and as such it is often depicted in the old tales as a magical beast, which is constantly reborn however many times it is eaten. In Ireland, at each of the hostels of the Otherworld gods, there would be great cauldrons filled with boiled or roasted pork, supplied by pigs who were continually reborn after each slaughter. In the father-god Dagda's *sidh*, or fairy mound, there was an unending supply of drink, three trees which perpetually bore fruit, and a pig that was always alive to provide food.

THE PIG AS NOURISHER

The pig as a gift from the gods or the Goddess to nourish humankind was clearly recognized by the Celts. They farmed pigs to such a degree that, the classical writer Diodorus Siculus noted, "they have such enormous herds of swine that they afford a plenteous supply for salt meat." These herds were allowed to forage in the woods, keeping down unwanted shrubs and undergrowth. In the spring and autumn they were turned on to the fields to manure and break up the soil.

Because of the pig's importance to the Celtic way of life, it was honored and respected, and was also used ritualistically. At the late Iron Age shrine at Hayling Island in Hampshire, large numbers of pigs have been found buried, and the shrine at South Cadbury in Somerset is connected to an avenue of burials of young pigs, calves and lambs. At the burial site of Skeleton Green in Hertfordshire male pigs were found buried with the men, while the women were buried with birds. A similar connection between male burials and pigs has been discovered in France, and the four columns of the inner sanctum of the Romano-Celtic temple at Hockwold in Norfolk rested on pig and bird bones—perhaps echoing this association of male with pig and female with bird. At the great Druid center of Chartres in France a young pig has been found ritualistically interred in a pit, and at Winklebury in Hampshire a pig and a raven were found buried together in a ritual shaft.

These pits or shafts were used to make thanksgiving offerings and were symbolically associated with the Underworld. The pig as a primary source of nourishment meant that it was a central feature of both the earthly Celtic feast and the Underworld feast too. Many chariot burials in both Britain and France include entire pigs—undoubtedly to ensure the soul's nourishment beyond the mortal realm.

GRANDMOTHER PIG

As a source of nourishment, the pig represents the Goddess, and in parts of the Scottish highlands a brood-sow is termed *Sean-mhair*—grandmother. As evidence that Druidry was perhaps originally Goddess-centered, Druids were referred to as "piglets" and the Goddess was sometimes pictured as a sow. One of the early Welsh Triads, *The Three Powerful Swineherds of Britain*, talks of the sow Henwen, the White Ancient, who gives birth to a wolf-cub, an eagle, a bee, a kitten and a grain of wheat. Henwen was said to possess great wisdom, having eaten the nuts which had fallen from the beech—a sacred tree of the Druids symbolizing ancient knowledge and tradition. Also within Welsh mythology, Ceridwen, responsible for the initiation and transformation of Gwion Bach into the magical bard Taliesin, is known as the goddess of pigs and barley. She manifests sometimes as a pig, her neophytes being addressed as piglets, her worshipers as swine, her Druid as boar or boar of the trees and her Hierarch as swineherd.

A pig is completely omnivorous—it will eat virtually anything it finds. But this lack of discrimination is balanced by the pig's ability to find hidden treasure, and pigs have been used to discover truffles and other fungal delicacies for centuries in Britain and Europe.

The ability of pigs to discover the earth's secrets is one of the reasons why the pig is so important in the Druid tradition. Both male and female pigs are sacred to the Goddess—the sow representing her life-giving aspect, the boar symbolizing her life-taking aspect. To fully understand the role of the pig as a totem animal we must study and work with both sow and boar.

BULL
Tarbh

Wealth, Potency,
Beneficence

The card shows a bull roaring, with three cranes circling in the air above, and with the leaves of a willow tree in the foreground. Two Celtic monuments, carved in the first century, both show a bull with three cranes and a willow tree. The cranes in the card remind us that, although the bull is an animal representing the earth, he is also linked with the sky and the heavens. We see the bull's testes which remind us of the association of the bull with fertility and virility. Early Druid shaman-rattles were shaped in the form of bull's testes, and one is shown lying on the grass. To the left we see a Bronze-Age Druid horn, whose sound mimics the bull's roar.

Tarbh mediates the influence of Taranis, the Jupiter-like god of the Druids, whose beneficence and expansiveness can bring you the opportunity for a rich and abundant life. The Bull is a symbol of wealth and as such it is auspicious to draw this card when considering financial matters. But remember that the ancient ones were wise enough to understand that true wealth is to be found in the heart and the soul first, and only then in the material world. The Bull represents fertility, potency, abundance and prosperity, but these things can sometimes take a while to achieve. If you need to work steadfastly in trying circumstances for a considerable period of time in order to achieve your goals, the bull will help you to do this without becoming drained or depressed.

Drawn reversed, this card may indicate that you are having difficulty in feeling motivated. There is no animal more stubborn than a bull who refuses to move, and it may be important for you to look at the roots of your lack of motivation — you may be making more of a choice about life than you believe. You may also need to ask yourself whether you are sufficiently sensitive to others' needs. Do you perhaps act like "a bull in a china shop" when confronted with certain situations? A bull's power when harnessed or channeled can be awesome, but when a bull is maddened he can become dangerous. You may need to attend to the way in which you react under provocation, and the way in which you might be tempted to use your personal power as "power over" others.

The Tradition of the BULL

I am a bull of seven battles
The Song of Amergin

The Celtic inhabitants of Britain were cattle-people. Cattle were central to their economy and their way of life, and the number of cattle owned was an indicator of wealth. The bull in particular became associated with the concept of wealth, both in its financial and in its wider sense: indicating power, prosperity, and fertility. The bull appeared frequently on Celtic coins, and a trace of its early association with prosperity lingers in our use of the term "a bull market" to describe a rising stock market. A further link with prosperity comes from the bull's association with the Celtic god Taranis, a god of thunder and lightning, oak trees and the Wheel of the Seasons or Stars. Taranis is a Sky Father god of beneficence and plenty, comparable with Zeus and Jupiter.

The central role that cattle played in the life of our ancestors meant that the health and fertility of the herd were of vital importance. Fertility was understood in its broadest sense to include an abundance of crops and livestock, creative works and children. Animal seed, crop seed and human seed were not seen as separate and independent, but as interdependent facets of Mother Nature's fertility, the fate of each inextricably bound up with that of the others. Bulls, in their castrated form as oxen, provided early communities with their power supply, pulling the plow and drawing water. In Britain and Ireland bronze horns and rattles were used in Druid ceremonies to summon the spirits and induce awe in the participants. Both these instruments indicate the reverence that was paid to the bull as a sacred animal. The horns were shaped like cow's or bull's horns and emitted a powerful rich note, with a few harmonics—sounding like an Australian aboriginal didgeridoo. The rattles, known as crotals, were bronze imitations of the bull's scrotal sack, with pebbles or balls of clay inside. Some are empty— perhaps designed to be struck, or to act as symbols of infertility to counterpoint the sounding rattles, which were clearly used as musical demonstrations of fertile power.

Although a bull is most clearly an "Earth" animal, his horns form the shape of a crescent moon, and point to the sky, connecting him to the stars. And they are used as ceremonial drinking cups to this day in Druid ceremonies.

THE TAIN BO CUAILNGE—THE CATTLE RAID OF COOLEY

In the Irish tale *The Cattle Raid of Cooley*, we read of the struggle between two supernatural bulls: Findbennach (White-horned of Connacht) and Donn (Brown or Lord) of Cuailnge in Ulster. Queen Medb and her lover Ailill, while lying in bed one night, boast of their possessions. They discover that they are both equally rich, but that Ailill also owns a magnificent white-horned bull. Medb then tries to buy the equally splendid Donn, but being refused, declares war on Ulster—to try to obtain him by force. The war culminates in a battle between the two bulls themselves. The Donn of

Ulster wins the battle, killing Findbennach, but then dies himself—having gone mad, killing all who crossed him.

The two bulls were once divine herdsmen in human form as the pig-keepers, Bristle and Grunt. They were "skin-changers," shape-shifters, arch-rivals who fought as ravens, stags, water monsters, human champions, demons, and finally eels. They were then swallowed by cows and reborn as bulls.

THE RITUAL SACRIFICE OF BULLS

In the early Irish ritual of *Tarbhfhess* ("bull sleep") the king of Tara was chosen in the following way: a bull was ritually slain, and a medium ate the flesh and drank the broth in which the meat had been cooked. As the medium slept, wrapped in the bull's hide, a truth-spell was chanted over him by four Druids, and a dream-vision was given in which the rightful king appeared.

The slaying of bulls was clearly deeply significant to the Celts: the Gundestrup cauldron shows three bulls being killed, and it seems that at some times "gateway ceremonies" were performed which involved the sacrifice of bulls, and their burial by the entrance. At the Gaulish sanctuary of Gournay the evidence shows that the animals were old—ten years or more—before their slaughter.

In Scottish tradition, to dream of a bull was said to be a sign of help about to arrive, and in Pliny it is recorded that two white bulls were ritually slain at the foot of an oak tree, when the mistletoe was cut from its boughs by the Druids. A memory of this archaic rite may linger in the naming of great hollow oaks in England as "Bull Oaks." But country folk say that they are so-called because bulls shelter inside them—in this way bringing together two of the major symbols of the god Taranis: oak and bull.

GOOSE
Gèadh

GOOSE

Vigilance, Parenthood, Productive Power

The card shows a pair of greylag geese in the fens. Ancestor of the farmyard goose, the greylag mates for life, and was once the only goose that bred in Britain. It may have earned its name from the observation that it "lagged behind" when other species migrated, although its name is more likely to mean "gray-legged." In the foreground we see bramble and gooseberry growing, with goosegrass to the right, and *Ngetal* (reed) in the background. In the sky a flock of geese are flying in V formation, heading out toward the sea.

Drawn upright, this card may indicate that you are ready to take on the responsibilities of raising a family, or of committing yourself to a long-term partnership. Gèadh brings creative and productive power. It allows you to open to this power, secure in the knowledge that your relationship or family or working partnership will provide a stable environment to act as a crucible for your creativity.

Raising children is one of the most joyful and worthwhile activities we can undertake, and the goose, with its strong attachment to its family, combined with its ability to fly extraordinarily high from one continent to another, shows us that it is possible to be both grounded and spiritual in our daily lives.

Drawn reversed, this card may indicate that you need to be aware of being overly concerned about your rights, possessions or territory. You may not need to strut and hiss quite so much, and you may not need to be so possessive of your partner. Many geese mate for life, but not all humans do, and in the end staying together may not be in your best interests. If the relationship is really to last it will thrive on mutual respect and freedom, rather than jealousy and possessiveness.

The ancient Celts kept geese for their eggs rather than their flesh. They knew it was better to keep the goose alive and productive, rather than destroying its productive capacity by eating it. They kept sheep in the same way—for their wool and milk rather than their meat. The lesson for us is that if we want to ensure our productive power, our capacity for creativity, we must look after ourselves. To make sure the goose keeps laying the golden eggs, we must keep the goose alive—well fed, well rested, well exercised.

The Tradition of the GOOSE

Swarms of bees, beetles, soft music of the world, a gentle humming; wild geese, barnacle geese, shortly before All Hallows, music of the dark torrent
Irish tenth century

It is said that the Druids of old were expert at divining from the flight of birds. As well as their psychic abilities, they would also have been using their skills as keen observers of the natural world. The arrival or departure of migrating geese, for example, would have given warning of the coming of winter or summer, and because of this the goose has come to symbolize seasonal change. And if wild geese were seen flying out toward the sea, it was taken as an augury of good weather, while if they flew toward the hills, it was said that bad weather was on its way.

In the quotation above, the writer talks of the barnacle geese who arrive in Britain in October for the winter. Coming from the Arctic, their arrival shortly before Samhuinn (All Hallows) would have been a powerful sign of approaching winter. Their origin being unknown, barnacle geese were said to hatch out of barnacles attached to driftwood, out of trees, or even out of acorns. In Scotland barnacle geese were sometimes called tree geese, since legend told that they came from willows on the Orkney Islands.

Samhuinn is traditionally the time of divination, but this period extends to fall generally, which is a season suited to introspection and reflection. The festival of Michaelmas represents the Christianized version of the autumnal equinox, and it was traditional to hold a goose feast, when the breast-bone called "Merry Thought" was examined and pulled for portents of the future. The pulling of the lucky wish-bone of the chicken is all that remains today of this custom, which may well have pre-Christian roots.

The goose feast also occurred at Christmas, and the goose signifies the renewal and purification represented by midwinter, when the sun is reborn at the solstice. Since the goose is a solar bird, laying the golden egg becomes a perfect symbol of this solar rebirth, with the mother-goose representing the Mother Goddess.

THE FIERCE GOOSE

Some of the strongest associations of the goose are with the qualities of aggression and defensiveness. The fact that the goose will vigorously defend her family and her territory, and that her loud honking gives ample warning of any visitor, has made the goose a powerful symbol of defensive power and guardianship. A great stone goose gazes watchfully from the lintel of the Iron Age clifftop temple of Roquepertuse in Provence, guarding a shrine of war-deities. At Dineault in Brittany a bronze figurine of a Celtic war-goddess has been found, complete with helmet surmounted by a goose in its characteristic threatening posture, with its neck thrust forward. And in the former Czechoslovakia, Iron Age warriors were sometimes buried with geese. Wild geese are good at flight as well as aggression—we still talk about a "wild goose chase" because they are notoriously difficult to capture and kill.

EROTIC POWER AND FIDELITY

The greylag, and other varieties of goose, mate for life and will fiercely defend their mate and their goslings, which, although ready to fly two months after hatching, will stay in the family for much longer. Complex courtship rituals and "triumph ceremonies" performed each time a pair meet have made the goose typify court-ship, partnership, and fidelity, although its preoccupation with mating came quite inappropriately to signify loose morals—a goose being a common term for a prostitute by Elizabethan times, and venereal disease being termed "Winchester goose." In reality the goose displays extraordinary steadfastness and devotion to one partner, but its pre-Christian depiction as a bird of creation and its related association with erotic power became distorted in the Christian period.

Although the Romans considered goose fat an aphrodisiac, the Celts used it for healing. On St. Kilda, in the North Atlantic, Britain's remotest island, it was called Gibanirtick and was greatly prized for its healing powers. With the first Christian missionary arriving only in 1705, St. Kildans retained their Druidic beliefs and practices well into the eighteenth century.

The goose with its strong attachment to its family combined with its ability to fly extraordinarily high, is a powerful symbol of the union of heaven and earth—and of the way in which we can unite both our spiritual and our everyday concerns. The American poet Mary Oliver expresses beautifully the ability of the goose to unite freedom and rootedness in this excerpt from her poem *Wild Geese*:

> *Meanwhile the wild geese, high in the clean blue air,*
> *are heading home again.*
> *Whoever you are, no matter how lonely,*
> *the world offers itself to your imagination,*
> *calls to you like the wild geese, harsh and exciting—*
> *over and over announcing your place*
> *in the family of things.*

RAM
Reithe

Sacrifice, Breakthrough, Achievement

The card shows a ram with an ewe and lambs in the background. To the left we see sheep-bit (sheep's kidney) and to the right sheep-sorrel. In the foreground grows stone bramble. A ram-headed snake is carved in the rock.

Reithe brings the ability to achieve a breakthrough. Particularly attached to the place of its birth, the ram represents connection, rootedness, stability, and yet it also represents the power to penetrate, overcome and achieve. Working with the ram as your ally will help you to find the inner strength you need to succeed. At the same time you need not fear "losing your head" on the dizzy heights of success, because the ram will help to keep you grounded, and will remind you of the practical necessities of life. By persevering, by being patient and attending to the needs of your daily life as well as your future goals, you will find the day comes when you achieve a breakthrough—accomplishing what you have set out to achieve and discovering that you have also "come home."

Drawn reversed, this card suggests that although a part of you may enjoy competition—locking horns with a friend or enemy—you may be called on to make a sacrifice. Sometimes letting go, however painful, can open the door to a new life that you never thought you could achieve. Rather than banging your head against a brick wall, see if it is possible for you to walk round it! Alternatively, it could be that you should be moving in a different direction, and the brick wall is there for a reason even if you cannot figure out why just yet. Ask yourself the question "Where do I feel really at home?" Follow your instincts and your practical nature to create a home around you that is truly comfortable and truly yours.

The Tradition of the RAM

Thursday, gentle Saint Columba's day,
The day to put sheep to pasture
Highland saying

The Celts kept sheep, primarily for wool and milk, but also for meat. Just as the tree was revered for the great contribution it made to humanity, so too were sheep, for all they gave. Both came to symbolize sacrifice, for the tree surrendered its life to give warmth, furnishing and shelter, having already given its shade, oxygen and fruit, and the sheep likewise gave up its life to give nourishment, having already given its coat and its milk many times. The god of the tree was known to Gaulish Druids as Esus at least two hundred years before the time of Jesus, and the fact that he too came to symbolize sacrifice may well point to a mysterious connection between Druidry and early Christianity, particularly since legend tells of the boy Jesus traveling with his uncle Joseph of Arimathea to Glastonbury, where, incidentally, wool was produced on a very large scale.

Although sheep were valued primarily for their live contribution to the economy, the ram was considered particularly suitable for sacrifice. Ram-roasting feasts were held near old standing stones in Devon at Beltane and on Midsummer's Day. The ram's throat would be cut as it was tethered to the stone, and dancing, games, and wrestling would follow the feast—with the meat bringing good luck to all who ate it. Nowadays such a festival is held at Kingsteignton on Whit Monday, but the ram is not slaughtered publicly.

The connection between rams and sacrifice is hinted at in Scottish tradition, according to which sheep once had the gift of speech. On leaving Paradise their last words were "do not burn our bones." In effect this meant great care had to be taken when roasting sheep and their bones were never cast into the fire. Firedogs were often wrought with rams' heads, and this may well represent an association between the animal and its sacrificial role.

When a sheep was killed, each part was allocated by tradition to a member of the household: the liver to the carpenter, the heart to the shepherd, and the shoulder to the astronomer. In ancient times, the astronomer may well have been the astrologer—the Druid or Ovate, who in Scotland, Wales and some parts of England used an ancient method of divination based on the scrutiny of the shoulder-blade of a sheep.

The tradition that sheep could talk may refer precisely to the fact that their bones "talked" in divination, and that their skin helped to make music—for both drumskins and the bags of bagpipes were furnished by sheep.

As well as providing music, sheep were also believed to offer considerable healing. Sleeping amongst them was curative if you had a lingering illness, their kneecaps provided a remedy against cramp, and for whooping-cough and jaundice a decoction of sheep's droppings was recommended.

THE TEACHING OF THE OPPOSITES

In the Irish tale *The Voyage of Maelduin*, the hero and his twenty companions find themselves visiting a series of magical islands, many of which are ruled over by animals. One of these is the Island of Black and White, with a brass fence dividing it in two. On one side is a flock of white sheep, on the other side a black flock. A shepherd throws a white sheep into the black flock and it becomes black. He then does the reverse, when a black sheep turns white. The story hints at a teaching about the nature of opposites, articulated most clearly in Taoist tradition, but also evident within much of Druidry. We are reminded, too, of the belief that a black sheep in a white flock brings good luck.

In another tale, *The Voyage of Teigue*, an island is discovered populated with sheep as big as horses. One flock is composed of huge rams, with one having nine horns. This giant ram attacks Teigue's men, but he kills it, and it takes twenty of them to carry it away. Another giant ram can be found in the old English folksong *The Derby Tup*, which describes a beast whose horns "grew so high, every time he shook his head they rattled against the sky." Describing its midwinter slaughter and the gifts it provides suggests that the song may relate to an old custom of ram sacrifice at the solstice.

THE RAM-HEADED SERPENT

A powerful symbol in Druid and Celtic tradition was the ram-headed serpent, a composite creature that we find depicted three times on the Gundestrup cauldron. In France there are bronze and stone sculptures of the horned god Cernunnos whose body is encircled by a pair of horned snakes, and these creatures are depicted on other Gaulish carvings in association with a goddess and a young man. In Gloucestershire there is an image of Cernunnos in which two ram-horned snakes make up his two legs, their heads emerging on either side of his head. These, and other images, suggest that the ram's head was added to the serpent's body to emphasize the power and penetrative nature of the masculine. Its association in iconography with solar and sky gods reinforces this interpretation. The ram was not used as a symbol of warriorhood. Instead, its connection with power, fertilization and healing was stressed by associating it with the snake.

HARE
Geàrr

HARE

Rebirth, Intuition, Balance

The card shows the original hare of Britain—the Arctic hare which was later replaced by the common brown hare, probably imported by the Romans from the plains of central Europe. It is nearly dawn but we can still see the moon in the sky. In the background stands a dolmen—symbol of rebirth—and in the foreground we can see a lapwing's nest, with the eggs which were said to have been brought by the hare. Harebell, hare parsley, and hare's foot clover grow close by.

Geàrr brings us the benefits of balance and intuition, of promise and fulfillment. The hare is a creature of the Goddess, the moon and the night, and yet it also represents the dawn, brightness and the east. It is the most adept of animals at shape-shifting: we can never be sure exactly where the hare is—in this or the Otherworld. It represents intuition, which makes things appear suddenly in our consciousness, like the lapwing eggs of Eostre, that magically appear in the hare's form (nest). As representative of the Corn Spirit and the two equinoxes, the hare brings the excitement of rebirth, fertile abundance and willing release as each creative cycle comes to an end. With the hare as your ally you will be well able to negotiate times of change, and you will be able to draw on your intuition to guide you through life.

Drawn reversed, this card may be suggesting that there is an imbalance in your life. It is possible that you are allowing yourself to be overly concerned with the Otherworld: regarding every unusual sign as a portent, or paying too much attention to "channeled" messages. To achieve balance, we need to concern ourselves with the outer realm just as much as the inner: of channeled messages someone once remarked, "Just because they're dead doesn't mean they're smart." Wisdom and guidance come from many sources, and you may need to apply common sense to a greater degree than you have in the past.

The Tradition of the HARE

Keen-eyed her hares and hounds,
Blackberries and fruit of the dark blackthorn
Weaving their wall in the woods
From "Arran of the many deer," Irish twelfth century

The hare's habits of foraging and mating at night mean that human observation of its behavior has until recently been severely limited. People once believed that hares changed gender annually, and that their frantic racing around and their peculiar boxing matches were confined to the month of March—hence the term "mad March hares." But we now know that this mating behavior takes place throughout the breeding season: before March it happens unseen before dawn, in March the days grow longer and they can be observed, but later in the spring the vegetation grows and their "madness" is again unnoticed by humans.

When her daughters were disinherited by the local governor, Queen Boudicca of the Iceni in eastern Britain led a revolt against the Romans which almost succeeded in destroying their power. The classical writer Dion described how she used a hare to divine the outcome of her first battle: "When she had finished speaking to her people, she employed a species of divination, letting a hare escape from the fold of her dress; and since it ran on what they considered the auspicious side, the whole multitude shouted with pleasure, and Boadicea, raising her hand toward heaven, said, I thank thee, Andraste [goddess of battle and victory] . . . I supplicate and pray thee for victory."

In the old days, hares were animals sacred to the Goddess—they brought luck, fertility, transformation, and healing. But as with other sacred animals, such as the cat and snake, Christianity degraded and inverted their symbolism. The close association between cats and hares is seen in their both having the nicknames of "pussy" and "malkin," and in medieval times it was commonly believed that witches could shape-shift or skin-turn into hares—to go milking at night, or to travel over great distances. It is possible that the "Hares' Parliament," in which hares sit in rings, reminded observers of the witches' circle, with each member of the ring being in reality a witch who had disguised herself as a hare.

A hare's foot was often carried as a protection against rheumatism, or by an actor to help with "shape-shifting" into a role, but in Scotland if a hare's foot was discovered on a fisherman's boat it was considered a curse, and the word "hare" was never to be spoken at sea. Similarly, seeing a hare crossing one's path when setting out on a journey was considered unlucky. It was also believed that the "machinations of the fairies"produced hare lips, or that in pregnancy the mother had accidentally startled a hare.

REBIRTH, RESURRECTION AND THE CORN SPIRIT
As bearers of good fortune, and as animals sacred to the Goddess, hares, or figurines of them, have been found buried in ritual pits. As a grave companion the hare is ideal, for it symbolizes the power of the Goddess to bring rebirth and immortality. This power is often represented in the Corn Spirit, who embodies the magical ability of the life-sustaining crops to die in the fall only to be reborn in the spring. The pagan underpinnings of Christianity become

abundantly obvious at *Alban Eiler*, the Spring Equinox. Here the hare is the original "Easter Bunny"—the word Easter being derived from the Saxon goddess Eostre, to whom the hare was sacred. Hares sleep outdoors in "forms," which look remarkably like lapwings' nests, and in spring when these nests are filled with eggs, it seems as if the hares have made them magically appear—they become the gifts of the Sacred Hare. As goddess, the hare has brought new life—rebirth—at the Equinox. The Christianized version becomes the moon-determined time of Easter, when the appearance of "bunnies" and chocolate or painted eggs marks the time of the resurrection of Christ.

The hare reappears again at the other side of the year—at the time of *Alban Elued*, the Autumn Equinox—when the promise of the spring is fulfilled in the autumn harvest. The last sheaf of corn to be cut was called "the hare" and its ritual cutting was known as killing or cutting the hare. If a hare happened to bolt out of this last sheaf as it was cut, this was considered extremely auspicious.

GRANDMOTHER HARE

Since the hare was sacred to the Goddess and symbolic of the Corn Spirit, eating it was taboo. In Kerry they still say that to eat a hare is to eat one's grandmother. But like horsemeat, hare's flesh was forbidden only in Britain and Ireland, except that the Kings of Tara were allowed to eat the hares of Naas. In Gaul the hare was the most popular of hunted animals. In Ulster "chasing the Cailleach" (the hag-goddess) was allowed immediately following the harvest, and in some parts of Britain hare-hunting was allowed on the one day of Beltane. Hare-coursing was a later introduction, probably of the Romans, but the image of the hare being pursued by the grayhound is powerfully invoked in the story of Taliesin—in which the fleeing Gwion turns himself into a hare to escape the goddess Ceridwen, who then shape-shifts into a grayhound to continue her pursuit.

Virtually impossible to raise in captivity, supremely fertile, the hare when caught cries like a human child. In the Western tradition, and in many other traditions throughout the world, it is strongly associated with the moon, whiteness, dawn and the east.

SALMON
Bradan

Wisdom, Inspiration, Rejuvenation

The card shows a salmon leaping toward a hazelnut that is falling from one of the nine trees of wisdom which grow beside the sacred pool. The Ogham sign for Reed—*Ngetal*—is carved on one of the nuts hanging near the water.

Bradan is revered as extremely sacred in the Druid tradition—it is the Oldest Animal, and it offers us wisdom and inspiration. Often with great difficulty, the salmon will return to the place of its birth to mate. To find wisdom, we too need to recapitulate our lives, to journey in consciousness back to our beginnings—to our childhood and perhaps beyond to our very origins in God or Goddess. Bradan brings not only wisdom but youthfulness and inspiration, but remember that to find these things you must maintain an attitude of openness and innocence rather than strong-headed determination.

Drawn reversed, the card may indicate that you are trying too hard to reach your goals, or that you are relying on someone else to find your wisdom for you. Contemplate the stories of Taliesin and Fionn mac Cumhaill and try to adopt a more relaxed and open approach to life. The salmon is able to jump upstream not by fighting against the current, but by utilizing its knowledge of the reverse current which flows beneath the surface current. From this salmon leaping we have derived the word summersault, as a corruption of salmon-sault. Children summersault, and choosing this card—reversed or upright—is urging you to connect with the leaping, dancing child within.

The Tradition of the SALMON

Peer often deep within the pool of Fec,
Peer often deep within the pool of thought,
And you will harmonize the wandering mind,
Recover sunken secrets of yourself,
Find love and light without you, as within,
And wake new wonder by the banks of Boyne
From "The Song of the Salmon-God" by W. P. Ryan

The Druid quest is a quest for wisdom and knowledge. This search leads finally to the Oldest Animal, Bradan the Salmon, swimming in the well of wisdom at the source of all life. In Irish mythology this well is called Conla's Well or the Well of Segais. It is the source of the River Boyne—that sacred river running through the Boyne Valley in which lie the ancient Druid temples of Newgrange, Knowth and Dowth.

This well or sacred pool has nine hazel trees growing around it, and it is their nuts which feed the salmon of the pool and render them wise. Even today we hear an echo of this ancient tradition whenever we talk about someone's head as a "nut." When King Cormac discovers the well, he describes it as: "A shining fountain, with five streams flowing out of it, and the hosts in turn drinking its water. Nine hazels of Buan grew over the well. The purple hazels dropped their nuts into the fountain, and five salmon which were in the fountain severed them and sent their husks floating down the streams."

The god Manannan explains this vision, and in his words we see how the Druid wisdom-tradition has survived to this day through such tales: "The fountain which thou sawest, with the five streams, are the five senses through which knowledge is obtained. And no one will have knowledge who drinks not a draught out of the fountain itself and out of the streams. The folk of many arts are those who drink of them both."

Here we are shown that knowledge is obtained through the senses, but also that we need to drink from the well itself—the well of inspiration. Not only does Druidry embrace the reality of the sensual world, it also recognizes the need to infuse our sensory experience with intuition and inspiration. Until we have come to the well and drunk from it, our lives are incomplete.

WHITE WISDOM AND THE FAIR ONE

In the Irish tale of Fionn mac Cumhaill ("Finn MacCool") we learn that a young man named Deimne went to the banks of the Boyne to learn poetry. He found there Finneces (White Wisdom) who had been seeking the salmon of wisdom for seven years. It had been prophesied that one day he would find the salmon, eat it, and know everything. He did indeed find the fish, and gave it to Deimne to cook, warning him to eat none of the flesh. But while he was cooking the fish, a splash of the boiling salmon juice burnt his thumb, which he immediately sucked. In this way it was the boy who received the salmon's wisdom. Finneces, the old poet, realized that it was the boy rather than he who had been the subject of the prophecy, and named him Fionn (The Fair One).

Across the water, in Wales, we find a remarkably similar tale. A boy named Gwion is set to watch over a cauldron in which Ceridwen has prepared a brew that will bring wisdom to her son Great Crow. A splash of the brew lands on Gwion's finger and in sucking his finger to cool it, he immediately knows all things. Furious, Ceridwen chases Gwion through many transformations until he disguises himself as a grain of wheat. She turns herself into a red hen and swallows him. When she subsequently gives birth to him, she ties the baby up in a leather bag and throws it into the river. Luckily Elphin finds the bag floating in the salmon-weir of his father, and rescues the child, naming him Taliesin (Radiant Brow).

In the stories of Taliesin and Fionn mac Cumhaill we see a common theme. In both stories the boys receive the prize of wisdom unexpectedly, whereas those to whom wisdom has been promised or prophesied fail to obtain it. The stories suggest that to gain wisdom we must not strive to achieve it head-on—wisdom comes unexpectedly to the innocent, to the humble, to the boy who is set to cooking or cauldron-tending, rather than to the person who is in charge and preoccupied with the search.

THE OLDEST ANIMAL OF ALL

The salmon itself was of such importance to the Druids that it can be found carved on the ancient Pictish stones in Scotland. It was said that since the salmon had eaten the magical hazel nuts, whoever ate the salmon would be inspired, and that these nuts were the cause of the red spots on its side.

In the earliest Arthurian tale, *Culhwch and Olwen*, Culhwch and his company are led to successively more ancient Totem Beasts until they find themselves face to face with the Oldest Animal of all—the Salmon of Llyn Llyw (The Lake of the Leader). The salmon, and only the salmon, is able to lead them to find the Mabon, the Divine Child of Druid Tradition—the Orpheus, Christ or Apollo being who brings eternal life and vigor.

The stories of Taliesin and Fionn connect youth with wisdom, and here again in the story of Culhwch and Olwen we see that youthfulness and wisdom are inextricably related—for we are not dealing with physical youth here, but youthfulness of spirit, a characteristic of the truly wise, at whatever physical age. We are also given a clue as to the means whereby the Druids worked to rejuvenate themselves, finding youth in old age just as youth can find the wisdom of old age. This work later came to be characterized as the search for the Elixir of Life, or of Eternal Youth.

BEE
Beach

Community,
Celebration,
Organization

The card shows a queen bee resting on a stone. In the background we see the House of Mead Circling at Tara as it may have looked at the height of its powers. In the sky the noonday sun shines brightly and we see *Ur*, heather, growing by the rock which is carved with the *Ur* Ogham.

Beach invites us to celebrate. You may have a special reason for celebration, or you may simply need to celebrate the wonder and mystery of being alive. You may like to enjoy a glass or two of mead, which—if it has been made in Scotland—will carry the scent of heather, and will bring you closer to the spirit of the Highlands. In the Druid tradition there are occasions to celebrate every six weeks or so. As human beings we need to have times when we can come together to enjoy each other's company. The bee tells us that we can live together in harmony, however impossible this may sometimes seem. By being at one with the natural world, by paying homage to the sun, by centering our lives around Spirit or the Goddess, we can work together in community.

Drawn reversed, this card may indicate that you are feeling out of place—unsure of your role in the world. A beehive functions harmoniously because each bee knows its role and the work it must do—consequently it is highly productive and plays an important role in the local ecology. We talk of a productive work environment as a hive of activity. If you find you are lacking in motivation, or are feeling isolated from the community that surrounds you, you may need some bee medicine. A modern English folk healer uses bee stings therapeutically to cure asthma and other ailments, and you may need to prod yourself into action before others do the prodding for you. If you find this applies to you, spend some time thinking about your role in life, and then make decisions in accordance with your sense of purpose and the resulting goals that this engenders. Remember that the bee knows the value of organization, of paying homage to the Goddess and the sun, and of working hard. Remember too that she calls us to a celebration of life and an inner recognition of our membership of the community of all Nature.

The Tradition of the BEE

Ask the wild bee what the Druids knew
Old English adage

In the Druid tradition, bees come from the paradisal world of the Sun and of the Spirit. Finely attuned to the position of the sun in the sky, it is the bee who brings the sacred solar drink of mead as a gift to humanity.

Mead is one of the most ancient alcoholic beverages in the world. Made from honey, water, malt, and yeast, it has almost certainly been brewed for at least six thousand years. It was, and still is, often drunk at the celebration of the eight Druid festival times, with the mead circling the participants until the last drop is consumed. At the royal court of Tara, the assembly hall was known as *Tech Midchuarta*, the House of Mead Circling.

The sun in the Druid tradition can, from one viewpoint, be seen as a manifestation of the Goddess, since in Celtic languages the word for sun was originally feminine—in Irish and Scottish it still is (*Grian* or *Griene*). The goddess Brighid is a goddess of the sun and of fire, as well as of wells and water. The firewater mead is therefore a most fitting drink to honor her.

THE GIFTS OF THE BEE

The bee's honey was only one of her gifts: she also brought wax for polishing and sealing. We cannot be sure that the Celts knew of the health-giving qualities of pollen and propolis, but we know of these now, even if science cannot enumerate the components of the anti-septic propolis, which bees smear on their hives to prevent infection, and which has been found to have remarkable healing properties.

It is likely, however, that every aspect of a bee's life was studied by the Celts and Druids. Nothing would have been ignored or wasted. The classical commentator Diodorus Siculus noted that, when the Celts washed honeycombs, they drank the washings. Meat was rubbed with honey and salt and cooked over an open fire. Salmon was baked in honey.

The Bardic Triads say that Britain was called the Island of Honey, and Ireland was celebrated for its swarms of bees and abundance of honey. In an early Irish text, the people of Munster were likened to bees, and it has been suggested that the mythical Queen Medb of Connacht may be associated linguistically with mead intoxication. When Medb, Maeve or Mab is seen as the Queen of Faerie, we can see how judicious draughts of mead might help the "second sight" or assist the celebrant's transfer to the faerie realms.

An Irish bard of the tenth century has written a lyrical eulogy entitled *The Hermit's Hut*. Its delights include "beer with herbs, a patch of strawberries, delicious abundance; haws, yewberries, kernels of nuts. A cup of mead from the goodly hazel-bush, quickly served; brown acorns, manes of briar, with fine blackberries." The writer shows us a world in which spirituality and sensuality, soul and body, have not yet been separated.

BEE

"I AM THE QUEEN OF EVERY HIVE"
The Song of Amergin

The gentle humming of the bee lulls us into sleep on a summer's afternoon. It draws us into the dreamworld—into paradise. The significance of the bee's hum is recognized in local common names for the bee such as the drumbee, drummer, doombledore, humma-bee and humble-dad. In the Welsh tradition a harp is known as a *teillinn*, a shortening or corruption of *an t-seillean* (a bee), and in one of the early Welsh Bardic Triads a magical sow, sacred to the Goddess and called Henwen, gives birth to a wolf-cub, an eagle, a kitten, a grain of wheat, and a bee.

The bee's extraordinarily accurate sun-dance in a lemniscate pattern is now understood as a means of communicating the orientation and distance of "rich pastures" to other members of the hive. Seen from the perspective of the Druid, the bees are engaging in a sacred dance of homage to the sun or the solar deity. Just as it is known that shamans would mimic the crane-dance, so it is also likely that Druid shamans would mimic the bee-dance, in celebration of the sun's life-giving powers.

The ancient Druid laws of Ireland, known as the Brehon Laws, protected bees and their hives, and on the Isle of Man it was a capital offense to steal bees. The hive itself was a symbol of the perfect community, and we see this image of perfection echoed in the beehive tombs or initiation chambers of Newgrange and Dowth in Ireland and in Spain and Portugal.

The bee, with its highly defined social structure and extraordinarily productive and efficient community, all centered around the Queen Bee, was seen as symbolic of the ideal society—centered on the Goddess, paying homage in sacred dance to the sun, and producing an amber substance from the flowers of the fields and woods that could both feed and divinely intoxicate.

OTTER
Dòbhran

Joy, Play, Helpfulness

The card shows an otter looking for salmon. A member of the weasel family, and a relative of the beaver, the otter is equally at home in water or on land. It is able to stay underwater for up to four minutes, and for safety the entrance to its riverbank home lies below the water-line. The otter uses its tapered, powerful tail as a rudder and as a tool when building, while its webbed feet make it a strong swimmer. Living mainly on fish, it is noted for its playfulness and sense of fun.

Dòbhran invites us to play, to "go with the flow" of life and experience—to become a child again. Allow yourself the freedom and pleasure of relaxing and letting go of all your daily concerns. Dòbhran could be prompting you to take a day or a weekend out of your usual routine—to do something purely for fun. Your practical self may tell you you cannot afford the time, but deep down you know that you need to take care of yourself to be of real value to others.

Someone may even be coming into your life who will show you how to play again—something you may have forgotten as you accepted the responsibilities of growing up. Dòbhran shows us that being playful can even lead us to catch the salmon—the fish prized by the Druids as the totem of wisdom. Drawing this card also confirms in us the sense that we are truly protected.

Drawn reversed, this card suggests that you may be "pushing the river"—going against the natural course of events, perhaps out of fear or stubbornness. Try letting go, relaxing and trusting in life. Although Dòbhran urges us to be playful, we must beware of becoming the playboy or girl who uses play as an escape from the demands and responsibilities of adulthood.

The Tradition of the OTTER

Glen of the sleek brown flat-nosed otter
leaping lightly, freely fishing
From "Deirdre Remembers a Glen," Irish fourteenth century

The otter is known for its strong sense of family—the cubs stay longer with their parents than most other young animals, and when an otter dies, its mate will often mourn for a long time. For these reasons, the otter has come to symbolize the strength of family ties.

The otter is sacred to the Irish god of the sea, Manannan mac Lir, and there have been a number of sightings of Otter Kings or "Master Otters." One was said to have appeared at Dhu Hill (Black Hill), waited upon by about a hundred ordinary otters. Another lived in Sutherland, and was completely white, although some said he was dun with a white star. In Scottish tradition, Otter Kings are brown, and are always accompanied by seven black otters as servants. When captured they would grant any wish, on the promise of release. Some preferred to kill them, for their skin when worn rendered a warrior invincible. Fortunately these otter kings were hard to kill: they could only be harmed if stabbed at one tiny white spot below their chin—a spot well guarded by their teeth.

THE STORY OF TALIESIN

Although sacred to a god, and having kings, the otter is also sacred to the Goddess. Ceridwen, the great Mother Goddess of the Druid tradition, pursued Gwion Bach as an otter-bitch when he tried to escape her by shape-shifting into a fish. During the time of Arthur, Ceridwen and her husband Tegid lived by Bala Lake. They had two children—a daughter Creirwy (Dear One) and a son Morfran (Great Crow). Great Crow was so ugly Ceridwen decided to consult the Books of the Pheryllt, the Druid alchemists, to see how she could brew a potion that would render her son all-wise, so that no one would care about his appearance, being dazzled instead by his brilliance of mind. She learnt that she should keep a cauldron of herbs bubbling for a year and a day, until three drops of Inspiration were obtained. She employed a blind man and his young assistant Gwion Bach to keep the fire stoked, and at the end of the year she and Great Crow sat by the cauldron ready to receive its first three drops. But they fell asleep, and as they did so three drops flew out of the cauldron and landed on Gwion Bach's thumb, scalding it. He quickly sucked his thumb and became possessed of all knowledge. Ceridwen, on waking, saw what had happened and began to chase Gwion in a fury. To escape her, he turned himself into a hare. To catch him, she skin-turned too, becoming a black grayhound. He ran to a river and became a fish, so she changed too, into an otter-bitch. He then turned into a bird, but she outwitted him by becoming a hawk. At the last minute he saw a heap of winnowed wheat, and dropping down, turned himself into a single grain. But the hawk-eyed Ceridwen spotted that grain, turned herself into a hen and swallowed it. Nine months later she gave birth to a son, who grew up to be the great bard Taliesin—Radiant Brow.

The English ballad *The Coal Black Smith* recounts a similar chase, but the male figure becomes in turn an otter, a grayhound, and a spider, whilst the female is a fish, a hare, and a fly.

THE OTTER AS FRIEND AND PROTECTOR

The otter and the fish are an ideal pair to symbolize the chase, for otters are excellent fishers. In the Irish tale *The Voyage of Maelduin* the seafarers toward the end of their journey reach the Island of Otters. There the kindly otters bring Maelduin's men salmon, just as they had been bringing fish to the island's sole inhabitant. Here the otter is portrayed as the friend of man, exemplifying the ideals of service, charity and helpfulness. Recognizing this quality of friendliness, many Celtic names for the otter include the word for dog: water-hound, brown-dog, water-dog, or sea-dog.

At home with the two feminine elements of water and earth, the sleek and graceful otter represents femininity, joyfulness and play. And like the toad, fox, and snake, the otter is said to carry a secret power object—a jewel or pearl within its head.

Otter skin was considered magical — it could be worn as a charm against drowning, it would keep harps dry when made into a carrying bag, and when lining the inside of a shield it would offer protection to the warrior. The magical powers of otter skin extended to healing: it was used as an antidote to fever and smallpox, and was helpful in childbirth. Whoever dared lick the liver of a recently killed otter while still warm, would receive the power to cure burns and scalds by licking them.

As well as offering healing and protection, the otter calls us to play, to relax in the knowledge that nature will provide for our needs, and that life can be fun and joyful. By taking ourselves less seriously, we will find that we can share with the otter the salmon of wisdom.

COW
Bò

Nourishment,
Motherhood,
The Goddess

The card shows a highland cow placidly standing beside the peaceful waters of a Scottish loch. In the foreground we see cow-berry (cranberry) and cowslip, and, to the right, milk-wort (field gentian).

Bò opens us to an awareness of the Goddess. Her generosity, healing and nourishing power is present all around you—in your friends and children, in your food and drink, in your dreams, and particularly in the natural world that you are blessed to live in. She brings protection from all harmful influences, and by attuning to her presence you can gain the inestimable benefit of deep and peaceful sleep. By opening yourself to Bò and to her sacred quality as a manifestation of the Goddess on earth, you will be connecting to the perpetual stream of nourishing energy that flows from the Goddess to each one of us. To experience this, there is nothing you need to **do**.

Drawn reversed, this card may be calling you to examine the ways in which you give to the world. If you believe your resources are limited, then you will be anxious about giving fully from your heart, but if you know that you are one with all of creation and all of nature then you will be able to give fully and freely. But you can only give if you are also able to receive. How easy is it for you to receive the love and concern of others?

The Tradition of the COW

Bees of small strength carry
The flower-harvest with their feet;
The cattle bring to the mountain
A rich-pouring abundance
Irish ninth century

Cattle are of such enduring importance to our well-being that they must have been given to us by the gods. Legends abound in Britain of sacred herds of white cattle, and Ireland was first gifted with cattle when three sacred cows rose out of the sea and came ashore at Baile Cronin. One was red, one white and one black, showing us that the cow is the Goddess herself—the three animals representing her triple aspect as virgin (white), mother (red), and crone (black). Although the gods did have cows—Manannan having sea cattle and the father-god Dagda a heifer called "Ocean"—they were more strongly associated with goddess figures, such as Boann— She of the White Cows—who gave her name to the river and valley of the Boyne in Ireland.

Brighid, goddess of the Brigantes tribe in north England, and one of the most important goddesses in Druid tradition, became the most commonly worshiped female deity in Ireland, transforming herself in Christian times into St. Bridget. Reared on the milk of an Otherworld cow, she took the cow as her totem, and was considered patroness of cattle.

The fact that the cow is considered sacred in India and was held in such reverence in Celtic lands adds support to theories of a common Indo-European ancestry. With its gifts of milk and leather, horn and meat, the cow was considered a source of nourishment on many levels. In healing, a cow's sweet breath was recommended for consumption, its dung as an effective poultice for burns and sores. Sleeping between cows was curative and warming, and if you needed protection from evil you simply had to go to a place out-doors where a cow had been resting, and lie there in safety, having cast a circle clockwise around this spot three times.

As they were sacred creatures vital to the human economy, three of the four Celtic fire festivals were related to them. The beginning of winter, at Samhuinn on November 1st, marked the time when the cattle were led down into the valleys and their winter quarters, and when the winter slaughter was carried out. At the opposite side of the year, at Beltane on May 1st, the summer began and the cattle were taken up into the high pastures, having been first led between the two Beltane fires to purify and invigorate them. The festival of Imbolc on February 1st marked the time of calving and lambing.

THE COW PATH OF THE STARS

Looking up at the night sky we see the bounty of the Goddess in the Milky Way—called in Friesland and Lancashire the Cow Path. And looking across the land we see how the old cattle droves once marked the main routes between centers of habitation.

The Celts determined a person's wealth by the number of cattle they owned. Rents, dowries, burials, even a bard's fee were pay-able in cattle. In Ireland an earl's son could be ransomed for 140 cattle, a king for one thousand. Cattle raiding or "lifting," as it was known in Scotland, was considered there a "creditable and gentle-manly practice." The associations to cattle in the Celtic mind are shown in the Irish word *tain* which means cattle and spoils and also mental endowments. The Irish *Cattle Raid of Cooley* was written on cowskin and was sung by dairymaids as they milked, for they knew that music and song made milking easier and increased the yield.

The cow as sacred to the Goddess was in close touch with the Otherworld. Scottish tradition tells of fairy cows (*Crodh Shith*) who live under the sea, feeding on seaweed, or who appear on land in special places—there are ten spots on Skye favored by them, for example. Some fairy cows were said to be the offspring of a water bull. In Ireland the first drops of milk were squirted on the ground as a gift to the fairies, and the use of milk as an offering is deeply entrenched in folk tradition. Some of the cup-marks on stones in Scotland were filled with milk for the "brownies" and in August milk was poured on hill-tops in Scotland as an offering to the gods. It was also believed that a fairy woman, the *gruagach*, would look after the cattle if milk was left out for her. In Brittany standing stones were periodically bathed in milk.

PROTECTING THE COW

The nourishing value of cow's milk, and its deep associative connection with mother's milk, was so respected that the cow needed to be protected from evil influences. If a cow fell ill it may have been struck by a fairy arrow, and a cure was to carry "need-fire" around the sick animal clockwise. The cow-fetter was ideally made with rowan twigs and stallion's hair, and its tethering rope, known as "the seal," was always included in the purchase price so that the magical protection of the seal remained unbroken. If a cow's milk would not make butter or had blood in it, it was said to be "blinked" or "eyed"—affected by malevolent forces—and steps were immediately taken to protect the animal. The herb ragfoot kept under a dish in the dairy would often prevent such attacks.

Milk was healing too. When the Irish were losing many men from the poisoned arrows of the British, the Pictish druid Trosdane told the Irish to fill a hole with the milk of 150 white-faced cows. The wounded were bathed in the milk and instantly healed.

And still today, whether she heals us with her breath or feeds us with her *bladhach*—blossom milk—the cow is the manifestation of the Goddess in the world.

HORSE
Each

The Goddess, The Land, Travel

The card shows a gray mare with the chalk hill figure of the White Horse of Uffington, Oxfordshire, in the background. In the foreground we see mare's peas (bog-bean) and horsetail growing, and, to the left, horse-shoe vetch. Carved on one rock is the symbol of a key, and on the other a mounted warrior. The sun is prominent in the sky above.

The spirit of *Each* calls us to journey, to travel. This may manifest itself as a desire to travel in the physical world, or we may be drawn to voyaging in the inner realms. She brings us energy and speed and connects us to the power of both the land and the sun. The horse-goddess is patroness of the complete life-cycle of birth, death, the afterlife and rebirth. By working with the spirit of *Each*, we will grow to feel comfortable with every aspect of the life-cycle, knowing that the goddess protects and guides us through each of its stages.

Drawn reversed, this card may be asking us to look at the roots of our restlessness. If we have difficulty settling down, staying in one place or completing tasks, it may be that we have not fully accepted the flow of the life-cycle and our part within it. Attuning to the spirit of the horse may help us to connect with our sense of place in the world—with the spirit of the land beneath us and the sky above us.

The Tradition of the HORSE

One horse was lithe and swift-leaping, high-arched and
powerful, long-bodied
and with great hooves. The other flowing-maned and shining,
slight and slender in hoof and heel
From "The Cattle Raid of Cooley"

These two horses drew the chariot of the Ulster hero Cu-Chulainn. Their names were Grey Sea and Black Seagull. Grey Sea was clairvoyant and when she foresaw her master's death she wept tears of blood. Cu-Chulainn rode into battle on a wood and wicker chariot, as many Irish and British warriors did long after chariot warfare had been abandoned elsewhere. The Celtic custom of headhunting in battle—fastening the enemies' severed heads to their horses' necks—must have made them terrifying opponents.

In pre-Roman Gaul and Britain the horses were small and pony-like, and they were used for haulage and hunting as well as battle. In Gaul they were also a source of food. Like sheep and cattle they were symbols of wealth, and the frequency of horse interments in ritual pits and chariot-burials points to their significance in Celtic life. Sometimes dogs and horses were buried together, which suggests a cult practice related to hunting, and at times horse-gear or simply parts of the horse, such as its teeth, are present as burial offerings. Horse bones have been discovered in the foundations of houses, undoubtedly to bring good luck, and the association of the horse with luck continues to this day with the belief in the horseshoe's ability to attract good fortune.

Since the horse is sacred and brings good fortune, it has to be protected from the evil eye with horse brasses. The Druids, and later country folk, would bless a horse by leading it sunwise three times around a cairn, which would be known as *Cairn Nan Each*. To protect a horse from theft by witches, carters would hang "hag-stones"—naturally-holed flint stones—around their horses' necks. The witches might then resort to throwing a magic bridle over a sleeping human—turning them into a horse for the night.

THE HORSE-GODDESSES

The horse-goddess Epona, from whom is derived the word "pony," originated in Gaul. But she was so popular that her cult spread to Britain and as far east as Bulgaria, and she became the only Celtic deity to be worshiped in Rome, with a feast day of December 18th. In Welsh tradition, her equivalent is Rhiannon, and in Ireland the goddesses Macha and Etain.

To cavalrymen the horse-goddess was undoubtedly a protectress, but to civilians she was the mother-goddess who presided over the life-cycle. In images of bounty and fertility she feeds two foals from corn in her lap. In other images she holds a key which unlocks the gateways to the Underworld or Otherworld. Shapeshifting into the form of a horse, she would carry the souls of the dead to the Summerlands or to Hy Breasil, the Irish paradise in the west, which some believe gave its name to Brazil. As horse of the dead, she is sometimes seen as a phantom creature or the provoker of nightmares. In Scotland the kelpie or *Each Uisge* haunts lochs and appears like a sleek pony, offering its back to travelers to help them cross the water. But once the victim is astride, it becomes a terrifying creature with huge teeth and long wild hair, and it plunges deep into the loch carrying its rider into the Underworld. In Skye it is said that unicorns live within certain lochs, and an eel-horse with twelve legs swims in Loch Awe.

THE GATEWAYS OF BIRTH AND DEATH

In the Druid tradition the time of Beltane, of mating, in May symbolizes the gateway for the soul to enter the world, and the time of Samhuinn, of death, at the other side of the year in November, symbolizes the gateway for the soul to leave the world. These two gateways act as fundamental points in the life-cycle. The horse-goddess opens the gates of life at Beltane, allowing in a great flood of ebullient energy which makes men feel like stallions and makes women refer to them as "studs." As the gates are closed at Samhuinn, she carries the soul to the afterlife, back to the Summerlands to be renewed again.

The association of the horse-goddess with the life-cycle of birth, death, afterlife and rebirth is confirmed when we discover that ritual Hobby Horses are ridden either at Samhuinn or Beltane. The Padstow and Minehead Hobby Horses bring in the May, while the Hodden Horse of Kent, the Wild Horses of Cheshire and Shropshire and the Mari Lwyd of Wales usher in the winter.

Being associated with the life-cycle and hence sexuality, the horse represents not only human fertility, but the power and fertility of the land itself. In Ireland certain kings undertook a symbolic marriage to a white mare to ally their own sovereignty with the power of the land. And as if to reinforce our awareness of the horse's connection with the earth, great images of the horse were carved on the chalk hillsides of Britain.

As well as symbolizing the power of the land, the horse also had a close affinity with the sun. As a solar animal, it was depicted pulling the sun's chariot across the sky, making it not only sacred to the Goddess but also to the sun and sky god. Whether allied with god or goddess, the horse provides us with the power and the ability to journey—in this world or the next. And with shoes, the horse can ride even faster and further. Horse-shoeing was first developed in the Celtic world, and the smith was considered an important figure: under old Welsh law it was he who took the first drink at any feast. And in Ireland the smith god Goibhniu was host at a feast which rendered his guests immortal. By taking us to Hy Breasil and back, the horse does indeed provide us with the means to transcend the limitations of mortality.

WREN
Drui-en

WREN

Humility, Cunning, God

The card shows a wren holding a feather in its beak, as it guards its nest filled with eggs. Tradition calls the wren's nest the "Druid's House." A bolt of lightning represents Taranis, the bull-god of thunder and lightning, the oak tree and the wren. The Ogham sign in the stone is of *Duir*, the oak.

Drui-en allows us to glimpse the beauty of God or Goddess in all things. He tells us that "small is beautiful," and that self-realization lies not in grandiosity or apparent power, but in humility, gentleness and subtlety. Cunning, if tempered with humor and good intent, is a way of achieving great things with an economy of effort, and a rational and honest use of the achievements of others.

Drawn reversed, this could mean that you need to look at whether your humility and gentleness actually render you invisible to others. Are they your way of defending yourself from life and from others, rather than facing life and its difficulties? Perhaps you also need to look at how you use your cunning, your native wit. It is easy for the habit of building on the work of others to become a dishonest exploitation of others' achievements, just as it is easy for cunning to become malign rather than benign. Remember that the story of the wren and the eagle can also be interpreted in a way that sees the wren as a cheeky and dishonest "upstart" who naively believes he can fool others and win status for himself through his ruse. Cleverness and building on the work of others require wisdom and honest skill if they are to be of value.

The Tradition of the WREN

A little bird told me . . .
Traditional saying

Of all the birds revered by the Druids, the wren was considered the most sacred. In Ireland it was called the *Drui-en*, or Druid Bird; in Welsh the word *Dryw* signifies both a druid and a wren.

Why is it that the Druid is pictured as an apparently nondescript little bird and not as an obviously powerful bird like the eagle? The following story from the western highlands of Scotland tells us. In a great assembly of all the birds of the air, it was decided that the sovereignty of the feathered tribe should be given to the bird who could fly the highest. The favorite was naturally the eagle, who immediately began his flight toward the sun—fully confident in his ability to win the title of King of the Birds. When he found himself soaring high above all his competitors, he proclaimed in a mighty voice his monarchy over all creatures that had wings. But suddenly, from out of his wings popped the wren, who had hidden himself under the eagle's feathers. He flew a few inches higher and chirped out loudly, "Birds, look up and behold your king!"

THE CUNNING WREN

This story shows us the wren as a cunning bird, prepared to build on the achievements of others and to mock their pride by outwitting them at the final moment.

The shaman was often known as the "cunning man," and the Druid-as-shaman is also the "cunning man"—the man who can become invisible like the wren, who can travel on the back of the noble eagle to reach his destination, saving himself energy in the process. Being small he is unobtrusive, and being small he can enter worlds that bigger people cannot—as Alice discovered in Wonderland. Being proud makes us unwieldy; being small and humble enables us to slip through the eye of a needle or down the root of a tree.

The Breton Druids go even further in according the wren a key role in their bird-lore: they say that it was the wren who brought fire from heaven, but that as she flew back down to earth her wings began to burn and she had to pass her gift to the robin, whose plumage also burst into flames. The lark then came to the rescue, finally bringing the gift of fire to the world.

The Druid's house is the wren's nest—a place of comfort and safety, for another important symbol in Druidry is the egg. The Druid's Egg, made famous by Pliny's remarks, articulates the idea that in order to grow and change we need to go through periods of incubation—withdrawing from the world to allow ourselves to re-form in the womb of time. The wren's nest was said to be protected by lightning. Whoever tried to steal wren's eggs or baby wrens would find their house struck by lightning and their hands would shrivel up. Lightning was considered by the Druids to be the weapon of the thunder bull-god Taranis, who often inhabited oak-trees, and the wren was sacred to Taranis. The oak struck by lightning is the symbol of the enlightened Druid—the sage infused with the power of the Sky Father. The Pictish stones found in Scotland often bear the zigzag line of a lightning flash to convey the same concept.

HUNTING THE WREN

On the Isle of Man a story is told of a fairy-girl or mermaid who lured youths into the sea. One of them threw a spear at her, and to avoid it she turned herself into a wren, but she was obliged to assume her own shape on each New Year's Day. On that day she was at the mercy of her hunters, who, if they were able, could kill her. A wren's feather became a lucky charm to preserve sailors from drowning, and no Manxman would go to sea without one.

The tradition of wren-hunting took place on New Year's Day until the Feast of the Wren was transferred to St. Stephen's Day on December 26th. With this tradition the wren has become a god or king rather than a mermaid—for the wren was hunted and killed in a ritualistic way, enacting the idea that the death of a god bestows strength on his killer, a variant of the belief that in the killing of the old king, his powers will be passed on to his successor.

In the unpleasant custom of hunting this tiny bird we see a distortion of an ancient Druid tradition. The wren symbolized wisdom and divinity. It is difficult actually to see a wren. At New Year the apprentice Druid would go out by himself into the countryside in search of hidden wisdom, in the same way that a Native American would go on a vision quest. If he found a wren he would take that as a sign that he would be blessed with inner knowledge in the coming year. Finding a creature small and elusive to the point of invisibility was a metaphor for finding the elusive divinity within all life.

At some point, with the transition from paganism to Christianity, that divinity once found was killed, as Jesus had been killed in Jerusalem. Christian tradition in the British Isles and in France is full of folk-customs surrounding the hunting of the wren, its procession in the streets, the singing of "The wren's knell" and other dirges, and its ritual buryings.

Part of the work of Druidry today lies in going deeper than our Christian heritage to reclaim the beauty and the life that our pre-Christian ancestors saw in Nature and all her creatures.

WATER DRAGON
Draig-uisge

WATER DRAGON

Passion, Depth, Connection

The card shows the Stoor Worm, a great sea-dragon whose "head was like a mountain and his eyes like round lochs, very dark and deep." Living off the coast of northern Scotland, he could only be appeased with the offering of seven virgins, bound hand and foot and laid on a rock beside the shore each Saturday. A young man called Assipattle killed him by riding a boat into his body and setting fire to his liver. As the dragon died, the crashing of his tongue made the Baltic Sea. As his teeth fell out, they made the Orkneys, the Shetlands, and the Faeroe Islands. Finally, he coiled himself up tightly and crashed into the sea—and old folk say that Iceland is his body, the liver still burning beneath its smoldering crust.

The Water Dragon brings that which is hidden into the light of day. Memories and wishes, which may have long lain forgotten or repressed in the Unconscious, may emerge to frighten or overwhelm you with their apparent negativity or destructiveness. Facing these experiences with compassion and courage will, in the end, bring you to an experience of a greater depth of soul and a greater sense of connectedness to all life. Although you may at times feel overwhelmed with emotion, with time you will be able to achieve a sense of balance and stability, as these strong feelings are integrated in your consciousness.

Drawn reversed, this card warns us to approach an exploration of our psyche and our past with caution. The conscious self can absorb the impact of only a limited amount of repressed or unconscious material being released into awareness. It is wise to work fractionally, little by little, to integrate unconscious material into consciousness. It is often best for healing and wholeness to be achieved slowly. Beware also of allowing your emotions to rule you in a way that later you will regret.

The Tradition of the WATER DRAGON

> One Sunday morning Lambton went
> A-fishing in the Wear,
> And catched a fish upon his hook
> He thought looked verry queer,
> But whatten a kind of fish it was
> Young Lambton couldn't tell;
> He wouldn't fash to carry it home,
> So he hoyed it in a well
> *From "The Lambton Worm"*

Just as life is said to have arisen out of the primal depths of the ocean, so too did the dragon begin its life as the Worm—a large snake or eel-like creature, sometimes horned, that would live in wells or lochs or the sea. Later in its mythological development, the Worm grew small wings and two feet and became the Wyvern, finally transforming itself into the fully-fledged Dragon with four feet, larger ribbed wings and a barbed tail.

Some Worms leave their watery habitats to coil around hills and terrorize the countryside, but others remain in the water and are depicted as sea or water monsters, the most famous living in Loch Ness. The first encounter with this creature on record tells of St. Columba saving a friend who was swimming across the river Ness. As the monster broke the surface of the water behind the swimmer, and opened his mouth wide with a great roar, Columba shouted, "Go thou no further nor touch the man. Go back at once." And the creature obeyed.

The Loch Ness monster is not unique: the whirlpools of the River Taff at Cardiff and Llyn-y-Gader lake in Snowdonia are renowned for their worms or water dragons who quickly devour anyone unfortunate enough to fall in—leaving the swirling waters blood-red within minutes.

THE LAMBTON WORM

Other Worms migrate from the water to land. The Lambton Worm of County Durham, immortalized in the folksong quoted above, was first discovered by Lambton as a boy, when he was fishing in the river Wear. Contemptuous of his catch, which turned out to be a strange eel-like creature, he threw it in a well, forgetting all about it, until years later he returned from the Crusades to discover that the Worm had "grew and grew so lithlie and so strong" that he no longer lived in the well, but at night "crawled about to pick up bits of news," and "if he felt dry upon the road he milked a dozen cows." After he had feasted on calves and lambs, children and sheep he would crawl away and lap his tail ten times around Lambton Hill.

Lambton had a special suit of armor made, with the front and back studded with steel blades. He then stood on a rock in the middle of the river and blew a horn, waking the Worm, which had been coiled asleep on the hill nearby. Slithering down to the river, it wound itself around Lambton, trying to crush him. But the blades cut and tore at the Worm, who fell in pieces into the river.

GATEWAYS TO THE OTHERWORLD

Whether the dragon is fully-fledged and fire-breathing, or is more primal and worm-like, there is a significant preponderance of water in all its forms—river, well, pool, lake, marsh, bog, and sea—in most dragon stories. Water, and in particular its sources, was sacred to the Druids, who also considered such places gateways to the Under or Otherworld. Since the dragon is an Otherworldly creature, it is fitting that it should emerge from such a gateway. In psychological terms, water represents the Unconscious and the emergence of monsters or dragons from sea, well, or lake represents unresolved complexes, repressed and distorted drives and desires, welling up into awareness. The destructive water dragon symbolizes perfectly the damaging nature of certain contents of the psyche, which, for the healing of the self, require a transmutation that may be depicted as a symbolic death.

For well over a thousand years such a destructive dragon was said to have lived in a pool called Knucker Hole at Lyminster in Sussex. Fed by a strong underground source, the pool was thought bottomless (in reality it is about thirty feet deep) and the home of Knucker the Dragon. By night he would go hunting in the marshy Arun valley, eating horses and cows, and finishing his meal by "sitting top o' Causeway, and anybody come along there, he'd lick 'em up, like a toad licking flies off a stone."

A local lad, Jim Puttock, baked an enormous and indigestible pudding which he fed to the Knucker. As it writhed on the ground with stomach-ache, he chopped its head off. The unmarked grave of Puttock the dragon-slayer can still be seen in Lyminster church. With the added effect of keeping children away from a local danger-spot, the tale combines an ancient mythological theme with local humor: "Sussex Pudding" was notoriously indigestible.

Earth and air dragons are usually harmless if not disturbed, and it is rare for the land or sky to present any great threat to us. But the elements of fire and water can indeed be dangerous, and the water dragon can overwhelm us with emotion and drown us in sorrow or self-pity. But if befriended, if related to as ally rather than enemy, it can bring passion, compassion, depth of feeling and a true sense of connection to all of humanity and the world of nature.

EARTH DRAGON
Draig-talamh

EARTH DRAGON

Power, Potential, Riches

T he card shows a coiled dragon guarding a hoard of treasure in its cave. An old inhabitant of the Welsh village of
Penllyne, who died at the turn of the century, insisted that his
father and uncle had killed such dragons. In his boyhood he
had seen them: coiled when resting, they "looked as if they
were covered with jewels of all sorts. Some of them had crests
sparkling with all the colours of the rainbow." When disturbed they glided swiftly, "sparkling all over," to their hiding places.

The Earth Dragon brings us face to face with our potential. Within
us we have a treasure house of riches—of powers and capacities—
which we can learn how to use. In the past we may have been
denied access by the guardian of this treasure. But now we are
coming to understand that this sometimes fierce guardian is in
reality an aspect of ourselves. By coming to know and love Draig-

talamh we will be able to unlock the secrets of our heart, and at the same time we will find ourselves discovering the beauty and the power that lie within the hearts of those around us and in the very earth itself.

Drawn reversed, this card may be indicating that somehow you are relating in an inappropriate way to your inner reserves and potential. Draig-talamh guards the treasures of your soul fiercely, but he is your ally, not your enemy—do not try to kill him, and do not try to wrest the treasure from him. You may need to spend time befriending this creature who has slumbered in your soul for so long. A precipitous attempt to capitalize on your talents or express your potential may be unwise.

The Tradition of the EARTH DRAGON

The dragon shall be in the tumulus, old, rich in treasures
Beowulf

At the foot of the great chalk figure of the Uffington White Horse in Oxfordshire lies Dragon Hill. It is said that St. George slew a dragon here, and to this day the ground is poisoned by the dragon's blood, which is why no grass grows on certain patches of the hill-top. Some have suggested that the stylized horse facing the hill is in fact a representation of the dragon. Whether it is or not, the fact remains that the dragon and horse share the same association with earth energy—with the power of the land.

Although some legendary dragons are strongly linked with only one of the four elements, many of them happily partake of the characteristics of all the elements: sleeping in water-holes, curling their bodies around hills by day, and flying through the air or breathing flames whenever they wish. Quintessentially alchemical, they speak of the energies and powers that exist both within our own selves and within the landscape around us.

That landscape is constantly changing, and some scholars suggest that the Druids practiced their own version of the geomantic art known in China as *Feng-shui*. This natural science of creating harmony in the landscape involves an appreciation of the earth currents or dragon-lines that criss-cross the land, and the art of knowing what physical features to add or alter to create the most harmonious atmosphere—one which is both esthetically pleasing and energetically beneficial. From this viewpoint, dragons become ley-lines or energy currents, and "taming the dragon" becomes a metaphor for practicing geomancy, or for the dowsers' technique of "earth-acupuncture"—driving iron stakes into the ground to control or divert harmful earth currents.

THE BARROW GUARDIANS

In ancient times, barrows and harvest hills, stone circles and single standing stones were raised with a sense of reverence for the land and with an awareness of its inherently spiritual power. When a barrow was filled with valuable grave-goods to accompany the dead warrior or chieftain, it is highly probable that the early Druids invoked spirit guardians to keep watch over the treasure, just as Egyptian priests invoked spirit beings to guard the treasures of the royal tombs and terrify potential desecrators. In time these guardians have become known as the monstrous dragons who so jealously guard their hoards at such barrows as the "Dragon's Hoard" in Oxfordshire, the Old Field barrows in Shropshire, the Drakelow barrows in Derbyshire and Worcestershire, and the "Drake Howe" barrow in Yorkshire. There is even a long barrow that is supposed to contain the bones of a dragon killed and buried there—at Walmsgate, a corruption of "Wormsgate," in Lincolnshire.

BURIED TREASURE AND THE INNER SEARCH

But treasure is not only found in barrows. Buried treasure within certain hills also has the benefit of a dragon guardian, such as Wormelow Tump in Herefordshire, and Money Hill on Gunnarton Fell in Northumberland. Under the Iron Age hill-fort of Cissbury in Sussex lies a hoard of gold, reached by way of a two-mile underground passage; but no one has ever succeeded in finding it because halfway along the tunnel two dragons stand guard.

The belief in treasure-guarding dragons is stronger in Wales than in England, although they tend to live in thick woods or on lonely hills, rather than in burial mounds or earthworks. An interesting feature of the tales concerning earth dragons is that unlike the air, fire and water dragons, they have minimal contact, if any, with human beings—no one tries to kill them and they spend no time devastating the countryside. Instead, they lie hidden and inactive unless disturbed. Although portrayed as having no trace of cruelty, like a slumbering volcano they carry the potential of threat and danger should they ever awake. Each of us has, perhaps, such a dragon guarding our inner riches. Concerned that none should violate the splendor of our innermost self, the dragon can sometimes deny even our waking consciousness access to these reserves of power and potential.

The earth dragon is found not only within the cave or center of the barrow or hill, but also curled around it. A powerful symbol of the journey of self-discovery and the spiritual quest is the maze or spiral form, which can sometimes be detected in the ridges found on the sides of certain hills such as Glastonbury Tor, or Bignor Hill in Sussex. In the legend of the Linton dragon, the spiral form of Wormington Hill was created when the dragon in its death throes coiled itself around the hill and contracted, squeezing it into its present shape.

There is a connection between the dragon that slumbers coiled around the hill or around the treasure in the cave of the heart, and the creature we discover at the center of the maze or spiral. Both are aspects of ourself—both can be seen as Guardians of the Threshold—to be respected and loved but also challenged and perhaps in certain senses overcome. Whether the maze is classical with seven rings, such as the sixth-century carvings found in Hollywood, Ireland, and Tintagel in Cornwall, or simply the triple spiral as found at the far more ancient sites of Newgrange in Ireland or Achnabreck in Scotland, it is generally agreed that such symbols represent the journey of the soul in and out of incarnation. If we can face the dragon-guardian of the treasure-house of the soul and Otherworld with sincerity and humility, it may well guide us through the labyrinth to the heart of the world, there to find the inspiration and the courage to be reborn again in time and space.

AIR DRAGON
Draig-athar

AIR DRAGON

Inspiration, Insight, Vitality

The card shows one of the dragons of Beli flying high over the magical city of Dinas Affaraon in Snowdonia. In the distance a bolt of lightning reminds us that Draig-athar is one of the servants of the Sky God.

Coming into contact with the air dragon can be as a bolt of lightning to the psyche and intellect—and as such must be treated with care and considerable respect. Sometimes manifesting as sudden flashes of illumination, Draig-athar brings insight and clarity to your thought and imagination. As conveyer of numinous power, the air dragon can be seen as a symbol of visitation—for he is a messenger of the Sky God.

Drawn reversed, this card may be indicating that you are in danger of becoming the servant of an idea, dogma or belief system. Contact with spiritual concepts and energies can sometimes stimulate the intellect in a way that produces inflation and delusion. To avoid this, constant reality-testing in the everyday world of relationships and practicalities is essential.

The Tradition of the AIR DRAGON

The gaunt wolf and winged serpent held
Dominion o'er the vale
Polwhele

Somewhere in the mountainous region of Snowdonia in Wales lie the remains of the ancient city of Emrys, home of the Druid alchemists known as the Pheryllt. In the Welsh tradition, this ambrosial city was also known as Dinas Affaraon—the "City of the Higher Powers." Here dwelt the dragons of Beli, one of the primal gods of Britain. The bard Taliesin describes one of these dragons in his poem *Protection of the Honey Isle*: "A deep cavern opens before me, shadowed by great rocks. The dragon comes out and crawls toward the cups of song."

From caverns high above the surrounding countryside the dragons would emerge to be harnessed to the chariot of the goddess Ceridwen. Most aerial dragons, though, are recorded as flying unencumbered and alone. In Devon it is believed that a dragon flies every night across the Exe Valley between the hill-forts of Cadbury and Dolbury Hill, guarding the treasures buried there. Also in Devon, flying dragons have been reported at Winkleigh, Challacombe on Exmoor, and near the tin-mine at Manaton. This last one, although only the size of a human, had a hiss that could be heard for miles around.

At Henham in Essex, a dragon eight or nine feet long with large eyes, fierce teeth and ridiculously small wings was sighted several times before flying into nearby woods, and in Somerset a fire-breathing dragon regularly flew across the marshlands from Curry Rivell to Aller, striking fear into villagers' hearts as they heard "the hiss of its wing-beat."

Some writers have suggested that the flight-paths of dragons represent the "dragon-lines" of earth-energy that run across the countryside—sometimes from sacred site to sacred site. Others have suggested that the bright heads and dark forked tails of comets passing close to earth became the flying fire-breathing dragons of folk myth. Tales of dragons could not have arisen from memories of the dinosaur age—sixty million years separates the last of the dinosaurs from the first humans on earth. But some stories may have been invented by smugglers to keep people away from their caves or forest hide-outs, and others may have originated when exotic reptiles escaped from private menageries. Still more tales may have been generated by authors or publishers duping a gullible public, and we do know of stories in which a dangerous boar or evil landlord has been portrayed as a dragon for added effect. But none of these explanations can adequately account for the universality of the dragon in the mythic and folkloric life of cultures all over the world—including the Druidic and Celtic.

DRAIG-ATHAR AS SERVANT OF THE SKY GOD

There is evidence, however, that some aerial dragons may be poetic or fanciful interpretations of unusual phenomena in the skies. Tornados can look uncannily "alive" and the dragons at Longwitton in Yorkshire and at Torrylin on Arran were both credited with being able to change into whirlwinds. AD 793 was described in a contemporary account as a year in which "came dreadful forewarnings over the land of the Northumbrians, terrifying the people most woefully. These were immense sheets of light rushing through the air, and whirlwinds, and fiery dragons flying across the firmament." A thousand years later, in Scotland, "many of the country people observed very uncommon phenomena in the air, which they call dragons, of a red fiery color, appearing in the north, and flying rapidly toward the east." Whether we believe these phenomena were in reality explicable in terms of meteors, ball and sheet lightning, the *aurora borealis* or UFOs, the fact remains that we cannot similarly explain the tales of earth and water dragons, or indeed tales of aerial dragons which are clearly not linked to celestial phenomena.

Such stories are to be found in Wales. At Penmark Place in Glamorgan people would often talk about the ravages of the winged serpents or dragons in that neighborhood. In the nearby woods around Bewper there was a "king and queen" dragon, and at Pen-llyne an old man, when interviewed in 1900, could remember them flying overhead "with outspread wings bright, and sometimes with eyes too, like the feathers in a peacock's tail." He insisted that it was true and "no old story invented to frighten children." Because they stole poultry, his father and uncle had killed several of them.

Within the Druid tradition, the flying dragon is a creature of the Sky God—coming perhaps from the constellation Draco, which turns about the Pole Star. He represents the descent of the spirit, a visitation from another world, an invitation to soar to higher levels of consciousness. Like lightning and thunder he can be terrible, bringing destruction in his wake. But treated with respect and gained as an ally, he can help us to travel in the spirit world—to journey ever further in the quest for enlightenment.

FIRE DRAGON
Draig-teine

FIRE DRAGON

Transmutation, Mastery, Energy

The card shows the flaming dragon of King Uther's vision. In the distance we see Glastonbury Tor. Legend tells of a secret cave within the Tor, used perhaps for initiation. Flaming dragons often guard such caverns, to prevent their desecration by the greedy and to offer their treasure to those who are worthy. In the foreground, lying on the rock, is a gold torc—a Celtic neck-ring indicating high status, rulership, and mastery.

Draig-teine brings vitality, enthusiasm, and courage, and an increased ability to overcome obstacles and to find the energy needed to cope with life's problems. Having the powerful Fire Dragon as an ally will align you with the qualities of leadership and mastery. With care, he will fuel your inner fire which can be directed and channeled with laser-like precision to help you accomplish tasks and achieve objectives.

Drawn reversed, this card suggests that you may be repressing a good deal of anger. This may make you feel that you are not in control of your life-energy. Either you experience this energy as out of control—erupting without warning or constantly bubbling near the surface—or you may sense it as scattered or dissipated. Are you often lacking in energy and vitality? Do you find it hard to get excited or motivated? Or do you find you have too much nervous energy, making you over-excited, unable to sleep, concentrate, or relax? Whether you have too much or too little energy, developing a harmonious relationship with the Fire Dragon will help you. If you are lacking in energy, you may need to ask the dragon to give you a little more of the treasure he is guarding. Or if you find your energy level is too high, you may need to do the reverse—to ask the dragon to take charge of some of your energy, guarding it fiercely, sure in the knowledge that you will be given access when you really need it. Draig-teine, like the volcano, can be dangerous, but if the inner rage that has been repressed for so long can be expressed and worked with, in a therapeutic setting, he can become a powerful ally.

The Tradition of the FIRE DRAGON

It is he who, blazing, seeks burial mounds,
He, the smooth, spiteful dragon that flies through the night,
Enveloped in flame; all men fear him greatly
Beowulf

King Arthur's father, Uther, at one time had a vision of a flaming dragon. This vision was so striking that he immediately asked his Druids to explain its meaning to him. They told him that seeing such a blazing dragon meant that he would become king. So he took the name "Pendragon," which means "Head of the Dragon." The dragon thereby became the heraldic emblem and totemic beast of the greatest line of British kings—the Pendragons.

This incident, which lies at the very beginning of the story of Arthur, provides us with the clue we need to understand the meaning of the Fire Dragon. Each of the four dragons of water, earth, air, and fire represents energy and power—but each mediates these in a different way, and eventually we will be called to integrate and weave together these four different types of "dragon energy" within our being. Fire Dragon energy is concerned with kingship, leadership, rulership, and mastery. And it is because of this that the Druids were able to interpret Uther's vision so accurately. It is said that his son, Arthur, wore a golden dragon on his helmet to symbolize his rank, and the fire dragon has continued to be a symbol of authority and power ever since.

MERLIN AND THE TWO DRAGONS

Legend tells that the Welsh flag, which shows such a dragon, has evolved from the time when King Vortigern found that he was unable to build his fortress at Dinas Emrys because the stonework of the foundations kept collapsing. Merlin, when still a young boy and known as Emrys, was brought to the court and he, with the aid of his mystical vision, explained that two dragons were fighting in a lake beneath the fortress, shaking its foundations. One was a red dragon, which represented the Britons, and the other was a white dragon, representing the Saxons. King Vortigern ordered the ground to be dug, to see whether Merlin was telling the truth; both dragons were found, and a battle between them began. The red dragon finally won and became the emblem of Wales.

Not all dragons are fierce or breathe fire. Earth dragons in particular are largely passive—sleeping coiled and inactive around or within tumuli or hills. But fire-breathing dragons are usually both active and fierce: including, for example, one that lived in the castle ruins at Newcastle Emlyn in Wales, and another at Challacombe on Exmoor; one terrorized the villagers of Bisterne in Hampshire, and two could be seen in Somerset—one at Kingston St. Mary and the other at Curry Rivell. At certain times this last one would fly across the marshlands to Aller, destroying all the crops and everything which met its fiery breath. An old account relates that "Milkmaids fled at the first hiss of its wing-beat . . . People lived in dread of a horrible death for themselves. At last a knight called John Aller came boldly to their rescue. He plastered his body with pitch and put on a mask so that the dragon's breath could not harm him." Arming himself with a spear he killed the dragon, although he died almost immediately after, burned by the dragon's breath. The spear he used to kill the dragon can be seen to this day in Low Ham church.

Nwyvre—The Dragon's Fire

The dragons of these folk tales are depicted as malign, but in the Druid tradition the fire dragon is seen as neutral—its effects are malign or benign according to our degree of preparedness. Not all knowledge is for public consumption, not all power is for use by all. The dangers of knowledge or power falling into corrupt hands are well known. The fire dragon is only malign when it is encountered by those who are unprepared or not sufficiently strong to handle the energies it represents—when it can bring "burn-out" and nervous exhaustion. The Fire Dragon guards the treasure of the Inner Fire that burns within each of us, and which is termed the Dragon's Fire or *Nwyvre* in Druidry, but which is more widely known under its Eastern name of *Kundalini*. This fire circulates through each of our psychic centers, or chakras, and its premature awakening through drug-taking or inappropriate esoteric techniques can lead to severe psychological imbalance and even physical illness. It is no wonder, then, that the Dragon which guards this force is pictured as fierce—for the consequences of misusing its power are grave indeed.

SEAL
Ròn

SEAL

Love, Longing, Dilemma

The card shows a gray seal on the shore of the sacred island of Iona, once known as *Isla Na Druidneach*, the Isle of the Druids. A pale rainbow shines over the Atlantic, and on the horizon we can see the outline of the uninhabited island called Dutchman's Cap.

Drawn upright, this card calls to you from the seal-people of the sea. The *Dan nan Ròn*—the song of the seals—upsets and frightens many who hear it. Its mournful and human sound stirs the heart of the listener to the core. It is a call from the sea, from the Unconscious, from the depths. It calls to us from the waters of our birth, from our beginnings on earth, from our brothers and sisters in the animal realm who are closer to us than we dare imagine. We fear this call, because we feel we may be drowned, overwhelmed by our feelings. But do not let your intellect imprison your heart, as the human imprisons his selchie spouse—the magical seal. Opening yourself to the promptings of the Unconscious, of the Feminine, of your dreams and longings will bring transformation, healing and love into your life.

Drawn reversed, this card suggests that you may have come to a time in your life when you are faced with a dilemma. Each way you turn could involve risk and potential loss, and yet you know you must make a choice. The seal speaks of the longing of the heart, of true love, of a sense of humanity and goodness. In the end, these should be the determining factors in your choice. Although the seal may represent loneliness and separation, as the selchie imprisoned on dry land, remember that the time will come when she will be released and will act as a guide and companion through the watery realm of the emotions and the Otherworld.

The Tradition of the SEAL

Look far off to the north-east
On the ocean so splendid
Teeming with life
Home of the seals
Shining and playful in the full tide
Irish ninth century

Seals have a strong and special connection with the human race. Some families are said to be descended from the union of humans and seals: in particular the Clan MacCodrum from North Uist and the Coneelys, Cregans and Hennessys from Ireland. The O'Sullivans of Co. Kerry also have seal ancestry, as do the MacNamaras— their name means "sons of the sea-hound." To determine whether seal blood runs in someone's veins, you should examine the rock where they have sat: "for no matter how warm the day, and his clothes being dry upon him, when he rises, there the rock will be damp where he was and the vapor from it lifting will leave crystals of sea salt beneath the sun" (from *The People of the Sea* by David Thomson).

In those places where seals are common, such as the Orkney and

Shetland Islands and the west coast of Ireland, many tales are told of the creatures which once provided meat, oil for lighting and medicine, and sealskin for waterproof boots and clothes. Although these local communities hunted seals, there were many traditional warnings that to kill a seal brought great misfortune.

Stories abound of seals helping humans—giving them rides, bringing fish as gifts, or saving those who were shipwrecked or half-drowned. Good luck followed those who helped the seals, just as those who harmed them were cursed with bad luck.

By far the most prevalent belief was, and perhaps still is, that some seals could turn themselves into human beings. In the Faeroe Islands they believed this skin-turning usually occurred at Midwinter, in the Orkneys it happened "at the seventh stream"—the seventh day of a nine-day period of high tides occurring twice a year, in March and at Lughnasadh in August. Another time for such an event was at Midsummer, known in the Druid tradition as *Alban Heruin*, the Light of the Shore.

The shoreline represents the magical boundary, constantly shifting like the tide, between this world and the Otherworld. For the Druids and Celts the sea is one of the ways of approach to the Otherworld, and from it certain seals, known as selchies or silkies, emerge at these special times to become partly human for a while.

"WOE BETIDE THE PERSON WHO WOULD STRIKE ME, FOR I AM A GENTLEWOMAN FROM ANOTHER LAND"
From the Songs of John MacCodrum

A tale is told in Ireland of a man called Declan who fell asleep on the seashore one morning, after having spent the early hours collecting crabs and cockles. He awoke to the sound of strange, haunting music and was astonished to see twelve people holding hands in a circle, swaying and singing. In the center of the circle stood an old man. When their singing stopped, they took off their shimmering silvery cloaks, leaving them on a stone, and then paired off into six couples and went to different parts of the beach to make love. Declan ran over to the stone and took one of the cloaks, for they were extremely beautiful. A while later, the couples returned and retrieved their cloaks, all, that is, except for one woman. She looked anxiously around, until she saw Declan standing in the shadow of a rock. Unafraid, she held out a webbed hand to him, explaining that she was one of the seal people, the last of the Ròn, and that once every hundred years they came on land to conceive children like themselves who could move between the worlds. Without her cloak she could never return to the sea. Declan brought out his knife, determined to have his way with her, but an old bull-seal came to her aid, striking and biting him, leaving him unconscious on the sand. The following summer, whilst crabbing at low tide, Declan went out too far—and, slipping on some rocks, by chance he was drowned.

THE SELCHIE SPOUSE

Other stories tell of selchie women who mate with men, who then hide their skins from them. They have children and raise their family until one day they discover their hidden skin in a chest or hayrick and are then faced with the awful dilemma of whether to return to their families at sea—for they often have seal-children too—or whether to stay on land. But the call of the sea is the stronger, and they put on their skins and hurry back to the ocean. Often, though, they will promise to keep their human children in fish, and will leave a supply each evening on a nearby rock. Variants of this story make the husband the selchie, and sometimes the children themselves become seals. An Orkney ballad, *The Grey Selchie of Sule Skerrie*, begins "I am a man upon the land. I am a selchie on the sea."

Some say the selchies are the enchanted children of the King of Lochlann, and in Ireland there is a legend that the seals were first created when a man called Kane was obliged to mate with nine hundred and one women in order to retrieve a particularly fine cow from the god Balor. He needed one child to help him in this task—the other nine hundred he cast into the sea and they became the first seals.

CHAPTER THREE

HOW TO USE THE CARDS

Wisdom of serpent be thine,
Wisdom of raven be thine,
Wisdom of valiant eagle.
Voice of swan be thine,
Voice of honey be thine,
Voice of the sun of the stars.
Scottish Gaelic Blessing

Serpent and Z-rod carved on a stone, from Aberdeenshire

The Animal Oracle does not predict the future. Instead it offers ideas and suggestions which may provide you with insights into your own life or the events surrounding you. These insights can help you take responsibility for your life rather than passively accepting your "fate" or "destiny."

Before working with the Oracle, it is important to know that your mental and emotional state at the time you use it will affect the outcome. This is for three reasons. First, when you start to use the Oracle you will need to ask yourself, or the Oracle, a question. The sort of question you ask and how you formulate it will vary according to how you are feeling at the time. Secondly, the way you interpret the answer you receive will depend on your mental and emotional state. Thirdly, there is undoubtedly an interplay between your unconscious and the Oracle, and your unconscious deeply affects and is affected by your thoughts and feelings. It may even be that your unconscious knows the answers you need and guides you to pick certain cards.

For these three reasons, it is important to use the Oracle when you are feeling reasonably calm and clear-headed. Interpreting the cards and applying their meaning to your life or someone else's life requires skill, intuition, and common sense. If you are feeling upset or distraught, you may pick on one or two words or phrases in the written interpretations and take these as the absolute truth rather than interpreting them in the context of your life. If you do this, you must take responsibility for this and know that you are doing it—not the Oracle.

At the beginning you will probably rely on the interpretations given in this book. But as you learn of the tradition surrounding each animal, as you meditate on each card, and meet—perhaps—the animal itself in your dreams and visions or in everyday life, you will come to your own sense of the card's meaning, with the result that you will not be dependent on the interpretations given here.

STARTING A READING

To get the best from the Oracle, make sure that you use it when you are able to be reasonably detached and objective—so that you can weigh its words against your own intuition and knowledge, and so that you can note the relationships between the cards given in the spread. Some people like to spend a few moments settling themselves and getting into the right frame of mind before using an Oracle—perhaps lighting a candle and letting go of everyday cares and concerns for a few moments by taking several deep breaths with the eyes closed. A Druidic way of doing this is to sense the earth beneath you—allowing yourself to develop a strong sense of connection with it, and then becoming aware of the sky above you while focusing on your breathing. You can then open yourself to feeling the earth's energy and the sky's energy meeting in the center of your body (which is usually felt as the Solar Plexus). After a while, open your eyes and begin the reading.

SACRED SPACE—THE DRUID CIRCLE

The circle is of immense significance in Druid teaching. In Druidry, all of life, including that of the earth and of our individual selves, is viewed as cyclical. Druids meet and work in circles, and the circle becomes a sacred space into which Spirit is invited and from which the Druid may journey in altered states of awareness. Various attributes are given to different parts of the circle, which represents both our own self and the horizon around us. Some of these attributes are given below, and full details of the richness of the Druid conception of the circle is given in *The Elements of the Druid Tradition*.

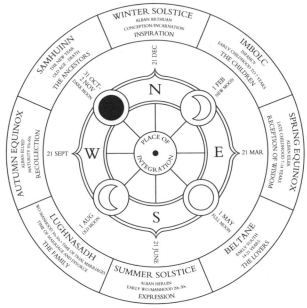

The Druid Circle

Certain places on earth have been considered sacred sites for thousands of years—in Britain alone there are the remains of over 1,000 stone circles. But we can also create our own sacred circle at any time—in our home or garden. Laying the cards in a sacred circle will allow them, over time, to become imbued with a power and an ability to awaken your intuition.

ASKING THE QUESTION

It is important for you to formulate a clear question in your mind before consulting the Oracle. It is tempting to skip this part, but if you have trouble formulating a question, ask yourself why this is. Maybe you do not have a question but just want some advice or guidance. That's fine—a request for advice is your question! But often there will be something worrying you, which is why you want to use the Oracle, and this initial stage of formulating a question is an integral part of the process of consulting the Oracle—it will help you to clarify your concerns, and it will also help you to interpret the cards more accurately.

SHUFFLING THE PACK

Pick up all the cards and remove any blanks. Turn half of them upside down and then shuffle the pack well, while holding the question in your mind. By using reversed cards as well as upright ones, the Oracle has the ability to give you sixty-six readings rather than thirty-three. Some people worry that reversed cards are "bad" or "unlucky"—this is not the case with the Animal Oracle. In most cases a reversed card simply offers more challenge than one which is upright.

CHOOSING THE CARDS

Now either spread all the cards face downwards in a row, like this:

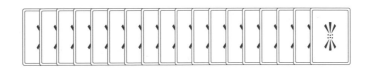

Or holding the pack in your left hand, cut it from the bottom of the pack twice to the left, forming three piles—1, 2, 3, and then re-assemble the complete pack from right to left—1, 2, 3, so that 1 is now the top third and 3 the bottom.

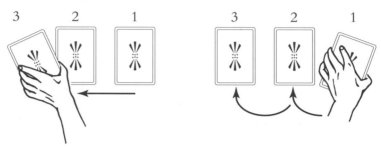

The left represents the Unconscious, and in most people the left hand is controlled by the right, more intuitive, side of the brain. In some people (usually left-handers) the reverse is the case and they might prefer to use the right hand, cutting the pack to the right.

With the first method, you can now choose cards one at a time from the row spread in front of you, to build up the spread. With the second method, you can lay the cards out in the sequence required for the spread starting with the top card and working down through the pack.

Both methods allow moments for the Spirit or your Unconscious to choose the right cards: with the first method during the selection of each card from the row, and with the second method during shuffling and cutting—with the exact places where the pack is cut being decisive.

THE SPREADS
WORKING WITH ONE CARD

The simplest way to work with the Oracle is to shuffle the pack as described, and then to pick just one card. Your question as you shuffle and pick the card may be a general one, as simple as "May I receive some inspiration for the coming day?" or it may be as specific as "What is it that is holding me back?" or "What aspect of my life do I need to look at now?"

Working with one card at a time is an excellent way to develop a familiarity with the sacred animals and their meanings, and can also be used to provide insights for a daily meditation. After you have read the interpretation and the pages recounting the sacred lore associated with that animal, see if you can open yourself to any message the animal may want to convey to you personally. Gazing at the card, or visualizing the animal with eyes closed, you may be able to smell it, to feel it breathing, to touch its fur or skin or feathers. Gradually you will develop a relationship with each of the animals, and your readings will become more complete and intuitive as they become dialogs with the animal spirits, or, when using more than one card, a conference of animal guides.

The Triune Spread

To gain an overview of a situation, and to gain an insight into the reasons why it has arisen and its effects on both the emotional and the physical level, choose three cards and lay them out like this:

The first card represents the cause, dynamic, impulse, guiding idea, or motive behind a situation or event. The second card represents its effect at the emotional, social, or relationship level, and the third card represents its effect at the physical level of manifestation—in the body or the concrete, tangible world.

THE AWEN SPREAD

Awen means literally "flowing spirit" and is the Druid term for divine inspiration or blessing. This spread is a development of the Triune Spread and involves the laying out of nine cards to create the Awen symbol of three rays of light:

The cards are laid out in three lines of three cards as follows:

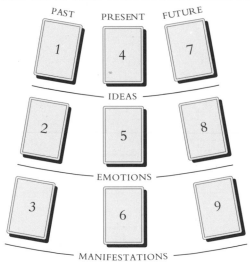

The left-hand ray represents the Past, the center ray the Present, and the right-hand ray the Future.

As in the Triune Spread the top cards represent the guiding ideas, causes, impulses, or dynamics, the middle cards the emotional effects, and the bottom cards the physical level of manifestation. It is best to understand the Triune Spread fully before working with the Awen Spread.

THE SPREAD OF THE ELEMENTS

To gain insights into those aspects of your self that may need developing or balancing, or which areas of personal development you may need to attend to, lay out one card representing your Self in potential, and four cards at each of the directions:

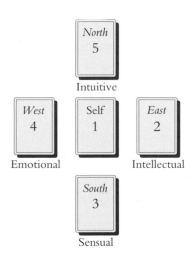

The card in the East relates to your intellectual, mental life. The card in the South relates to your sensual, instinctual life. The card in the West relates to your emotional, feeling life. And the card in the North relates to your intuitive, spiritual life. Look particularly at the relationships between the cards themselves.

THE SPIRITS OF THE CIRCLE SPREAD

Druidry recognizes the influence of six factors on who we are, and the direction we take in life.

Our genes clearly influence us, and this influence is represented in the sacred circle as the collective Spirit of our Ancestors. The culture in which we have been raised affects us powerfully too, and this is symbolized by the Spirit of the Tribe. The time we were born and the times we live in are significant factors too, and they are represented in the sacred circle as the Spirit of Time. Where we were born and where we spend our lives also influences us greatly, and this is represented as the Spirit of Place. All these four influences are particular to our present incarnation.

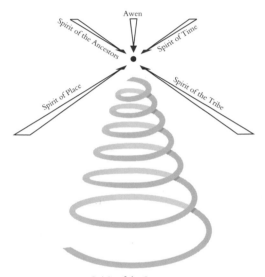

Spirit of the Journey

But we are also influenced by the accumulated experience of our previous lives. This influence is termed the Spirit of the Journey, and is sometimes sufficiently strong to override all other influences. Finally, despite these five influences on our characters and lives, there is the Awen—the "gift/blessing/grace of the gods" over which we have little control. (To learn more of this way of understanding the Self, see *The Elements of the Druid Tradition*.)

We can use the Spirits of the Circle Spread to gain insights into how we are being influenced in our life and how we may best make use of the gifts or challenges that have been given to us by each of these six forces. Lay out the cards in the following pattern in the order given, with the first card signifying your Self:

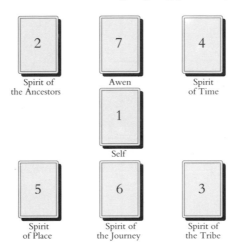

The first sample reading given (see page 164) will clarify the way you can work with this spread.

THE HEARTH SPREAD

Although you may use this spread to gain insights into any situation or event, it is particularly helpful in clarifying issues relating to the home or relationships. The layout is based upon the Druid symbol for the Spirit of the Home or Hearth, as found carved in Brittany (for more details see *The Book of Druidry*):

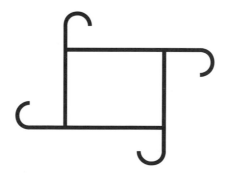

The cards are laid out as follows:

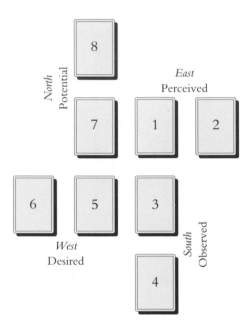

The positions represent the following aspects of the situation or question asked:

EAST   1 and 2   **Perceived**   The way you perceive or think about yourself or the issue.

SOUTH   3 and 4   **Observed**   The way you or the issue is perceived by others.

WEST   5 and 6   **Desired**   The way you want yourself or the issue to be.

NORTH   7 and 8   **Potential**   The way you or the issue could be.

The second sample reading given below will clarify the way you can work with this spread.

The Arianrhod Spread

Arianrhod is the Druid goddess of the wheel, the circle and the spider's web. The spider is a creature whose web symbolizes the Web of Life. Sacred to the Goddess, she represents the process of weaving—another idea that is central to Druid ritual and teaching.

In this spread, the first card—representing the Self—is laid in the center, and eight cards are laid in a circle around this, in a sunwise sequence that starts in the NW at the place of the Druid New Year, at Samhuinn.

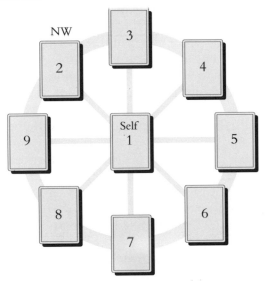

The reading may be used to gain insights for the year that is to come, or to review the year that has passed. It is ideal for an annual reading on one of the festival days, such as Samhuinn—a traditional time for divination. The sequence of eight cards may relate to a cycle of time other than a year. Imagining the cards spread upon a web or wheel, pay particular attention to the relationships between the cards.

INTERPRETING THE CARDS

To begin with, you will need to use the key-words and inter-pretations for each card given in Chapter Two. If you are interpret-ing a reversed card, read the first as well as the second paragraph of the interpretation. You may also like to read the reversed card's meaning even when you have drawn it upright—for sometimes it can represent a "shadow" or hidden side of the issue being considered.

One way of understanding the Oracle is to see it as an expression of the totality of your being and its potential. Like a diamond with thirty-three facets, each card can be seen as a symbolic repre-sentation of one facet—one part of yourself. When you do a read-ing, or a reading is done for you, a number of facets are highlighted, but it is important not to forget the whole.

Using a different image, one can imagine a stage with thirty-three actors representing different aspects of oneself. With any one reading, a group of actors is called on to the stage or steps forward into the spotlight, but the other actors are still there in the Theater of the Self.

Once you have read the key-words and interpretations, and re-lated these to their positions in the spread, take a while to look at any patterns or groupings that may exist. You may have a pre-ponderance of birds or animals related to one particular element or quality, for example. Or you may have related animals in signifi-cant positions within the spread.

A summary of groupings is given opposite. You may wish to add your own groupings or alter these groupings in accordance with your own intuitions and guidance.

Always leaving room for exceptions, it can be said that generally a preponderance of air cards suggests intellectual and mental issues to be considered, of water cards emotional issues or factors, of earth cards practical matters, and of fire cards issues of energy and will. If a number of dragons appear in one spread this may in-dicate a great deal of spiritual energy present in the issue being considered, and if a good many of the cards in a spread are re-versed, this may indicate a considerable number of challenges to be faced.

GIFT, QUALITY OR ABILITY

HEALING	ADDER, BOAR, DOG, FROG, RAM, RAVEN
PROTECTION	BEAR, BOAR, CAT, DOG, GOOSE, OTTER, RAVEN
FERTILITY AND CREATIVITY	ADDER, BULL, COW, GOOSE, HARE, RAM, SOW
SENSITIVITY TO THE OTHERWORLD	BLACKBIRD, CAT, CRANE, FROG, HARE, HIND, HORSE, OWL, RAVEN, SEAL, STAG, SWAN, WOLF
CONNECTION WITH FAERIE	CAT, COW, HIND, SWAN, HORSE
INITIATION	OWL, RAVEN
SHAPE-SHIFTING	CAT, HARE, HIND, SEAL, STAG, SWAN, WOLF
JOURNEYING	CRANE, DOG, HORSE, STAG, AIR DRAGON
PAIRS	COW AND BULL, BOAR AND SOW, STAG AND HIND, HARE AND CAT, DOG AND WOLF
ELEMENTS	**EARTH** DRAGON, ADDER, BEAR, BOAR, BULL, CAT, COW, DOG, FOX, HARE, HIND, HORSE, RAM, SOW, STAG, WOLF
	WATER DRAGON, CRANE, DOG, FROG, OTTER, SALMON, SEAL, SWAN
	AIR DRAGON, BEE, BLACKBIRD, CRANE, EAGLE, GOOSE, HAWK, OWL, RAVEN, SWAN, WREN
	FIRE DRAGON, ADDER, EAGLE, HARE

Depending on the spread, the relationships between certain card positions are significant, and it is worth noting whether you can sense any meaning from the cards drawn in these places, when considered in relationship. With the Awen Spread, you may be able to trace a relationship horizontally between the cards as well as vertically. Considered horizontally, you may notice a relationship between the causal impulses of past, present, and future; between the emotional states in past, present, and future; and between the three cards denoting physical effects.

In the Arianrhod Spread the cards opposite each other may be in relationship: the cards at Beltane and Samhuinn, for instance, or at the equinoxes or solstices. A knowledge of the Druid festival cycle will help when interpreting these.

The card placed in the center of the Elements, Spirits of the Circle and Arianrhod Spreads represents the Self. You may sometimes wish to place a blank card in this position or to use one with an egg drawn on it—a symbol used in Druidry to denote the Self with all its potential as it prepares to be born or reborn.

Finally: do not take the interpretations given for each card as the absolute truth—the final word. We have derived these interpretations from our knowledge of the Druid and Celtic lore related to each animal, a consideration of their characteristics and behavior in the natural world, and inner work. If you read the pages relating the traditional lore, and combine your understanding of this with your own inner work and knowledge of the animal concerned, you may well be able to refine and expand these interpretations. You may also be able to work with the images the cards evoke in you, and the associations the key-words and interpretations evoke. Further techniques of dialoging and identifying with the animals can provide even more insights.

SAMPLE READINGS
THE SPIRITS OF THE CIRCLE SPREAD

In this first spread, Kelly had no particular question for the Oracle. She seemed to have no pressing concerns in her life as a successful writer, but since she was very busy, she wanted to use the Oracle to gain a sense of where her life was taking her. As we asked her to formulate a question she realized that in fact she was feeling under a good deal of pressure, and eventually her question became a request for some insight into the forces that were causing her to feel this pressure—and how she might respond to them. We suggested the Spirits of the Circle spread, and the cards she chose were as follows:

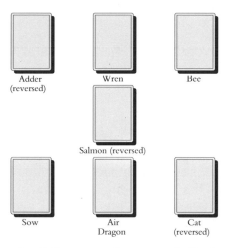

In the center was the Salmon card reversed. On hearing the interpretation, Kelly recognized that the search for Wisdom was central to her life, but realized that in its reversed position it was telling her that she was striving too hard to achieve this wisdom. She was pleased to find the card echoing her own sense that she needed to "connect with the leaping, dancing child within."

In the place of the Spirit of the Ancestors, reading the interpretation for the reversed Adder provoked tears in Kelly, and she told us that she experienced her relationship with her family as one in which she was continually hurt and wounded. She saw the need to transform that wounding into a healing, and understood that she was not simply a victim of the family but a part of it. Thinking further, she felt that the Adder was urging her to transform her relationship with her family—taking a more active and positive stance toward it.

In the place of the Spirit of the Tribe, which represents the influence of one's culture, Kelly had drawn the reversed Cat card. Having heard the interpretation, she responded by identifying the reversed cat as typifying the sixties culture she had grown up in, which had now become the "New Age" culture. While she recognized its positive contributions to the life of the Spirit, she saw that a part of its influence on her had been to seduce her away from the challenges of life by its preoccupation with "altered states" and other realities. She chose to accept the cat's positive influence, though, of detachment and the ability to survey important issues without prejudice, and of a sensitivity to both the physical and non-physical worlds.

In the place of the Spirit of Time Kelly had drawn the Bee card, symbolizing community, celebration and organization. After reading out the interpretation, we invited Kelly to ask herself how she felt the "spirit of the times" was inviting her to act in her life. Seeing the connection between the card she had drawn and our question she replied by saying that she felt she was being urged to organize her life and work while introducing into it times of celebration. She admitted that she often felt so busy or so driven that she had no time for socializing. Reading the interpretation again, and the pages relating the tradition of the bee, she realized that she had forgotten the spiritual dimension of celebration and socialization. She also felt that she was living at an exciting period in history—when the spirit of the times was urging humanity as a whole toward the concept of "community" in its widest sense.

The card representing the influence of the Spirit of Place was Muc—the Sow. At first it was hard for Kelly to see a connection between the place in which she lived and the interpretation given, but then she understood that where she lived was in fact an immensely nourishing place. Everything that she could possibly need, both physically and spiritually, was readily available in the small country town in which she had made her home. Because she was so used to it, it came as a surprise to her to experience it as a manifestation of abundance and the generosity of the Goddess.

Before looking at the influences of her previous lives and of the Spirit, we took a moment to look at the four influences we had just examined, in relationship rather than separately. Two reversed cards and two upright cards suggested a good balance of challenge and stability. The two cards on the axis of Time and Place were offering great support and encouragement—suggesting that her present circumstances and environment were acting in a positive and nourishing way. The two cards on the axis of Family and Culture—Ancestors and Tribe—were both reversed and offered more challenges. Here we were dealing with people rather than situations and circumstances, and Kelly agreed that she found relationships with both family and friends difficult and sometimes painful. When we asked her to think of associations to the four animals, she said that the sow and bee reminded her of summertime—of warmth, brightness, daytime, and the country. The snake and cat made her think of darkness, and threat, of stealth and hidden places. She then saw how she conceived of the place and time she was living in as bright and supportive, whereas her relationships were more of a mystery to her—carrying the potential of threat and the anxiety of the unknown and the unpredictable.

We then looked at the influence of the Spirit of the Journey, which was given as the Air Dragon card. Kelly immediately saw her inspiration and ability as a writer reflected in this card, and was pleased to find it in this position—confirming her sense that her vocation was central to her life and that she was drawing on talents that were not simply confined to this incarnation.

The last card, the Awen or "gift of the gods" card, was the Wren—bringing the blessings of humility, gentleness, and subtlety. The interpretation also spoke of the rational and honest use of others' achievements, which helped her to understand her role as a writer, who is often obliged to draw on the work of others for inspiration and information. For a long time she had had difficulty coming to terms with the fact that writers feed on each other's work, and by reading the reversed card's interpretation too she was able to make a clear distinction in her mind between the correct and incorrect use of other authors' work.

Looking at the three central cards in relationship, Kelly could see that her search for Wisdom, represented by the Salmon, was nourished by both the inspiration of the Air Dragon and the influence of the Wren, which would temper any tendency to inflation or grandiosity caused by the dragon's inspiration. By opening to the fact that she was inspired by the dragon and blessed by the gods with the Wren's qualities, she felt able to open to the dancing, leaping, summersaulting child within. This gave her the strength to face her relationship difficulties, knowing that she was being strongly supported by the times she was living through and her environment.

THE HEARTH SPREAD

In this second reading, Peter was concerned about where he and his family were going to live. He and his partner had moved ten times in the previous two years, and they were still not settled, even though they now had an eight-month-old baby. He was asked to hold this concern in his mind as he shuffled and cut the cards. Peter's cards were laid out as follows:

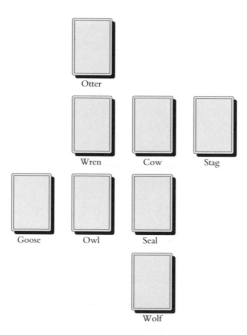

The reading given showed that the central issue that needed to be resolved in order for the family to find a permanent home related to

Peter's dual, and apparently opposing, tendencies and interests that, at an unconscious level, prevented a cohesive family unit developing. The Perceived pair of cards showed that Peter saw himself as both a Cow, mothering and "fussing" over his three children, and as a Stag, a creature which embodies and symbolizes pride, independence, and a connection with the Otherworld. His difficulty came from reconciling his need for both independence and a family life.

Peter confirmed that he perceived himself in this way, and that the two main concerns in his life were his children, toward whom he felt very protective, and his spiritual or "otherworldly" pursuits, which drew him to "journeying" away from home, either physically or psychically. He often perceived these two tendencies as contradictory, the Cow pulling him toward the hearth, toward the family and home, while the Stag urged him to be on his own, pursuing the Inner Quest.

The cards which represented the way Peter and his situation were perceived by others were the Seal and the Wolf. In the Scottish Highlands, it was believed that there was a certain kind of seal—the selchie—who could take human shape. Some men took selchies for wives, hiding their skins to prevent their escape. But when their wives finally found the skins they would leave home and return to the sea.

In this reading, the seal card represented that part of Peter which always appeared to his partner not fully present, but elsewhere—longing for the sea, the ocean of bliss, the Otherworld.

The Wolf symbolized that part of Peter which he sensed as the Stag, but which was perceived by his partner as "the lone wolf"—often wanting to be on his own, and appearing to defend his inner territory aggressively.

In the east, Peter perceived himself as a Cow and a Stag, in the west—the place that indicates Peter's desired qualities or situation—we see the cards of Goose and Owl. This suggests that he would like the qualities typified by Cow and Stag transmuted into the qualities of Goose and Owl. The Owl is the symbol of Initiation, Wisdom and Teaching. Peter hoped that his Stag, being connected with the Otherworld, might become the Owl—able to impart his knowledge of the Otherworld as Wisdom. The Cow in the east becomes the Goose in the west—the mothering, nurturing qualities of the cow changing to the qualities of parenthood, productive power and vigilance. In discussing the difference in feeling between goose and cow with Peter, it emerged that he felt that he was too "motherly" with his children, and longed to be more "fatherly." The goose suggested to him that he should focus on parenthood rather than trying to follow traditional models of motherhood or fatherhood. The fact that the goose is also associated with creative power clarified for him his sense that part of his creative energy was bound up in being motherly. He felt that by applying the qualities of vigilance and discipline typified by the goose, he might become more creative as he became a more effective parent.

In the north, we find the cards of the Wren and Otter indicating Peter's potential. Both animals have a quality of lightness and playfulness about them that is in strong contrast to the more serious feelings conveyed by the Owl and Goose.

The Otter is seen by the Druids as a friend of man, typifying the qualities of joy and playfulness. Although he swims in the water, he is able to form the same strong bond of affection with a human as a dog. For this reason, the Otter can be a strong ally. In this reading, the Otter seemed to be calling Peter to swim playfully and joyfully in the waters of feeling.

The wren is known in Ireland as the Druid Bird, and in Wales the word *Dryw* signifies both a Druid and a wren, and the wren's nest is called The House of a Druid. The wren symbolizes the knowledge that "small is beautiful" and that too much striving often hampers our spiritual search. It tells us we should not be afraid to build on the achievements of others: that we do not always have to go it alone and do it all ourselves.

Both Otter and Wren showed Peter that life can be fun and that he needed to take life less seriously.

Asked how the cards helped him to understand his original question, Peter was able to see how the inner conflict between his need for independence and a family life had been subtly blocking his attempts to find a home. He was surprised to realize that others saw him as a lone wolf, with an air of absence, but was pleased to learn of his inner desire to transmute his qualities of otherworldliness into wisdom and the desire to teach, and into a more balanced style of parenting. Finally, with the cards in the north, he was relieved to discover that the way forward to uncover his potential lay in becoming less serious and more playful. He decided to commit himself fully to his family, so that he no longer unconsciously sabotaged their attempts to settle down, and in a while they were able to find a permanent home.

Further Work with Sacred Animals

We had a rhyme for every bird when I was his age, and some of
the animals too, and every one had the right sound to it
From "The People of the Sea" by David Thomson

As well as using the Animal Cards as an Oracle, there are many other ways of working with them and the sacred animals they represent.

If you are feeling out of balance or in need of direction or guidance, pause for a moment and ask the sacred animals to present you with the gift you need. Then choose a card. The interpretation may provide you with insights or helpful advice, and the animal may be offering you its own "medicine" or energy which cannot be expressed in words. You may like to carry the card with you for a while, or to have it by your bed or somewhere where you will see it often. In this way the card will act as a link between you and the power animal, and it will also act on your consciousness through the process of subliminal suggestion—your brain will register its image and its associations subliminally many times each day.

If you need a particular gift or quality, you can choose the relevant card using your knowledge of the animal, or the key-words, or the guide given on page 163. Again, you can keep the card near you, and study the life and habits of the animal. If you felt in need of healing, for example, you could turn to the guide listing healing animals and choose one or more animals for attunement.

Reading the old tales, such as the Welsh *Mabinogion*, and the early Irish myths and sagas, will open you to the richness of the Celtic tradition, and will deepen your understanding of sacred animal lore.

As you start to work with the animals, you may feel drawn to one more than any others. This may indicate a natural affinity for it, and that it may wish to become your power animal or totem. Studying its characteristics and behavior, visiting it in the wild, joining conservation groups to protect it, drawing pictures of it or writing stories about it, will all help to make you feel closer to it. You may want to write a letter to it—which will prime your Unconscious and will also act as a symbolic gesture of communication, a reaching-out to it. You may meet its spirit in your dreams or in meditations or inner journeying. Sometimes you may feel drawn to merge with your animal and to move as it moves—dancing and singing in a way that will allow you to express the animal's energy in the world and which will enable it to fill you with healing and invigorating power.

SACRED ANIMALS EMPOWER US

"The role of the Power Animal has always been to link the human species with the larger collective environment or ecosphere. We are all part of each other. By dreaming of an animal, by performing a ritual, by retelling an ancestral creation myth, the Dreamer, the Shaman, the Bard is working with the essential unity of life, and can journey into the collective spheres of being, through the mediating role of the animal" *(Nicholas Mann)*.

As we work with the sacred animals of the Oracle, we need to ask whether these animals are in fact simply symbolizing parts of ourselves or whether they have an outer objective existence in another dimension. It seems that both are true. The animals can symbolize parts of ourselves—the bull or horse can represent our sexuality, the hawk or eagle our intellect, for example. In this sense they can be termed inner or subjective animals. But experience and tradition tell us that the animals also have an objective reality in the Otherworld. A great deal of pioneering work has been done by the psychologist Stephen Gallegos on the psychotherapeutic value of working with our inner animals—with our hidden fears, urges, hopes, and wishes which can be evoked and then related to as